Tony Gray is an experienced journalist, author and scriptwriter who started his career as a junior leader-writer at the *Irish Times* in 1940. Since then he has worked on various newspapers, including a spell as Features Editor of the *Daily Mirror*, and has enjoyed a successful career in television scriptwriting and production.

He is the author of over a dozen books including *Fleet Street Remembered*, a history of the Street incorporating the personal reminiscences of such famous old hands as Keith Waterhouse, Nigel Dempster, Jeffrey Bernard and Lord Rothermere.

He is married, with two grown-up children, and divides his time between Surrey and France.

From the library of
Danny Doyle
Raised on songs and stories

THE LOST YEARS

THE EMERGENCY IN IRELAND
1939–45

TONY GRAY

WARNER BOOKS

A *Warner* Book

First published in Great Britain by
Little, Brown and Company 1997
First published by Warner 1998

Copyright © Tony Gray 1997

The moral right of the author has been asserted.

A CIP catalogue record for this book
is available from the British Library.

ISBN 0 7515 2333 X

Typeset in Palatino by
Palimpsest Book Production Limited,
Polmont, Stirlingshire
Printed and bound in Great Britain by
Clays Ltd, St Ives plc.

*Cover picture: Known as the 'Carlow Panzers',
armoured cars built by a Carlow blacksmith
on a Ford chassis became a familiar feature
of the Irish landscape in 1941.*

Warner Books
A Division of
Little, Brown and Company (UK)
Brettenham House
Lancaster Place
London WC2E 7EN

CONTENTS

INTRODUCTION

The Final Emergency

In the wake of the celebrations for VE Day in 1995, I started to think about the war years in Ireland, possibly because that year, for the first time ever, an Irish Taoiseach (John Bruton) went, with Sir Patrick Mayhew, British Secretary of State for Northern Ireland, and with representatives of Sinn Fein, to a British Legion anniversary celebration in Dublin – in this case it was the 50th anniversary of the arrival of British troops in Belsen – at a period when the IRA cease-fire had held for almost a year, and permanent peace in Northern Ireland seemed a distinct possibility.

Previously, although about 50,000 citizens of the new Irish state volunteered for service in the British armed forces during the Second World War – and a number of the most distinguished commanding officers in all the services were Irish – both Government and Opposition deputies in the Dail were extremely reluctant to acknowledge that any Irishmen were serving or had ever served with any of the British forces during the conflict. This was one of the reasons why the word 'war' was studiously avoided in Irish political and government circles; it was always referred to as The Emergency.

Mind you, this was not a word with which the Irish were unfamiliar; it was a commonly-used phrase. The Irish Free State of 1922, born out of an emergency, had plunged itself into an even more profound one when the Treaty Settlement was rejected by de Valera and his Republican Irregulars, after it had been accepted by a narrow majority (64 to 57) in the Dail, the Irish equivalent of the House of Commons. The Civil War which resulted was clearly another emergency which could be solved only by elaborate emergency measures which, in effect, allowed the pro-Treaty Free State Government to lock up or liquidate large numbers of their enemies – their former comrades-in-arms in the struggle for freedom – on the pretext of protecting the national interest. By the time the Civil War ended on 30 April 1923, 77 'irregulars' had been shot, including Erskine Childers – who in a sense could be said to have started the whole fight for independence by running a consignment of German guns into Howth in 1914 – and about 12,000 of their comrades-in-arms were in jail. The British reprisals after the Easter Week Rising of 1916 had been trivial by comparison.

When de Valera was finally returned to power

in 1932 – as a result of a variety of circumstances which included Cosgrave's undemocratic, strong-arm methods of dealing with the continuing violence – one of the first things he did was to work out a new constitution for the entire 32 counties of Ireland, claiming the partitioned-off Six Counties of Northern Ireland over which the Irish Free State Government did not, for the moment, hold any jurisdiction, as part of 'Eire – or in the English language, Ireland', as the constitution put it. This understandably produced such a sharp reaction in Northern Ireland that for several years after his 1937 Constitution, de Valera was burnt in effigy by the Orangemen every 12th of July, the anniversary of the Battle of the Boyne, when the victory of William III over the Catholic King James II 'ensured forever the Protestant succession'.

The word 'emergency' had been used throughout The Troubles, throughout the Civil War, and constantly during the years when de Valera's new government was trying to cope with various attempts to make life difficult for him, coming both from his former comrades among the Republican Irregulars (the anti-Treaty section of the IRA), and from the more fascist remnants of the pro-Treaty National Army which had fought against them during the Civil War, among them General Eoin O'Duffy's Blueshirts.

But when the rest of Europe appeared to be on the brink of war in the late summer of 1939, the word emergency acquired a new and much more urgent meaning. Dependent as they were upon Britain for everything from coal and oil, tea and candles, pots and pans, to bricks and timber, nails and electric-light bulbs as well as motor-cars, tyres, batteries and spare parts, and even such primitive farm machinery as the Irish had learned to use, the war in which Britain seemed about to be involved became, for Ireland, the ultimate national emergency. Though this was not the aspect of the situation which most concerned de Valera in the initial stages of what became known simply as The Emergency.

On the week-end when the world went to war, de Valera told the Dail that his view was that a 'time of war', as defined in the Constitution, covered an emergency such as the country was now facing; the point he was trying to make was that the circum-stances constituted sufficient of an emergency to justify the introduction of Emergency Powers Orders for the protection of the State, even though Ireland was not going to be directly involved in the war that now appeared imminent. To do this it was necessary to amend Article 28.3.3 of the Constitution to extend the meaning of the phrase 'in time of war' to include: 'a time when there is taking place an armed conflict in which the State is not a participant but in respect of which each of the Houses of the Oireachtas (Par-liament) shall have resolved that, arising out of such armed conflict, a national emergency exists affecting the vital interests of the State.'

The acceptance of this final emergency allowed a new nation – which was always only too ready to accord itself exceptional and dictatorial measures for its own protection – to start paving the way for a series of Draconian Emergency Powers Orders which were effectively to abolish democracy for the duration. As well as law and order, the Government gave itself dictatorial powers over almost every aspect of the life of the country including censorship of the press as well as of private correspondence, military matters, supplies, power, fuel and transport.

It was a curiously claustrophobic period in which we were cut off, not merely physically but even more so mentally, from the main stream of world experience. I have called this book *The Lost Years* because for many people, in particular those of my generation, who were just in the process of becoming adults when the war broke out, they were lost years in a variety of different ways, though it could be argued that for Ireland as a nation the enforced isolation that resulted from the policy of neutrality proved in many ways a blessing in disguise. But the war years were certainly lost years for those of us who in other circumstances might have been lucky enough and sufficiently well-heeled to afford to sow a few wild oats abroad in Paris or London or Rome; in those days few ordinary people thought of venturing much further afield.

For the thousands of young Irish men and women who joined the British armed forces and survived, or who went to work in other capacities in the United Kingdom, the war provided an alternative opportunity to sample life outside Ireland's then oppressively constricting boundaries. But for others who, like myself, saw the logic in de Valera's decision to declare Ireland neutral in Britain's war with Hitler, and who decided for one reason or another to stay on there for the duration, Ireland became a prison camp, albeit a very pleasant one. We were all, in a sense, interned. We couldn't go anywhere. At one period of the war, we even needed a permit to cross the border into Northern Ireland, much less to cross the sea to England.

The one way to see a bit of the rest of the world during any war is to join the armed forces, but the Irish armed forces – only 7,600 strong at the outbreak in 1939 – clearly weren't going anywhere. And although during the course of the war about 50,000 young Irish people volunteered to join the British forces, and saw a great deal of the world, many more sincerely felt that if there was any danger of an invasion of Ireland, from any quarter whatsoever, it was their duty to stay on and join the Army, the Marine Service or the Army Air Corps, or at least volunteer for the Local Defence Force, a part-time reserve. In all, 250,000 young Irishmen and women enrolled in the Irish defence forces which, by the end of the war, had developed into a highly efficient army which has since provided very useful UN peace-keeping troops for Cyprus, Israel and the Congo.

While Britain was blacked-out and blitzed, life in Ireland went on in an almost defiantly normal way. There were shortages, of course, but in an agricultural country with a very thriving brewing and distilling industry, there was always plenty to eat and enough

Guinness and Irish whiskey to get drunk any time you felt like it. Cigarettes were a bit of a problem, it is true, but as nearly everybody knew somebody with a bit of a lean on somebody else working in a tobacconist's shop, nobody went seriously short of a smoke.

Gas was rationed, so were clothes, tea and sugar, and even bread for a time, and coffee was unobtainable. There was no coal; so we burned turf, a story in itself. There was no petrol, so we cycled to work and to the mountains and the sea and to the race-meetings, and to the dress dances held almost nightly in Dublin throughout the period. Horse-drawn vehicles were hauled out of their retirement homes in haylofts and barns and refurbished, and horses were taken off other duties to go between the shafts of traps, cabs, side-cars and carriages of all sorts. And while those few of England's small boats still in commission during the early years of the war were used to rescue the battered remnants of the British Expeditionary Force from the beaches of Dunkirk, yachting on a flamboyant pre-war scale flourished in Dublin Bay and elsewhere in Ireland throughout the entire period of The Emergency and there were extravagant regattas every other weekend during the sailing season.

There was relatively little unemployment, because there was always plenty of work going in the war factories of Britain; during the years between 1939 and 1945 – apart from the 50,000-odd young men and women who joined the British forces – between

25,000 and 50,000 men and women (again mainly the younger ones) left Ireland each year of The Emergency to find jobs in England, and few of them returned after the war. Many tens of thousands more went to the United Kingdom to work for short periods to earn a bit of extra money.

In December 1938, the IRA suddenly took it into its head to serve an ultimatum on the British Home Secretary, demanding the instant withdrawal of all British troops from Northern Ireland and threatening dire reprisals if the British refused to comply. This action was a direct result of de Valera's failure to secure any concrete concessions on the partition issue in his 1938 negotiations with the British, and it was supported by the surviving members of the second Dail – a ghostly assembly which, as I shall explain later, claimed to be the only true Government of the Republic of Ireland, and now 'handed over' its authority to the IRA Army Council under Chief of Staff Stephen Hayes – as well as by the Irish in America, in particular by Joseph McGarrity and his comrades in Clan na Gael.

The reprisals took the form of time-bombs left in letter-boxes and warehouses, railway station left-luggage departments and cinemas. Plans to disrupt English life by blowing up the public utilities like the gas and electricity power stations fell through and the amount of damage to life and property was not great, though a Scottish doctor called Campbell lost both legs in an explosion at King's Cross and another explosion in Coventry killed five people, wounded more than fifty and did thousands of pounds' worth of damage.

And a couple of days before Christmas 1939, the IRA raided the Magazine Fort in Phoenix Park and stole the bulk of the Irish armed forces' total supply of small-arms ammunition and a quantity of heavy explosives; although most of the stuff was soon recovered, the IRA remained throughout the early war years a thorn in de Valera's flesh, a well-armed (if not particularly well-disciplined) and very militant army, determined to continue the fight for the removal of the border; and – since they were initially in constant contact with German agents – they appeared to pose a grave threat to Ireland's policy of neutrality. Also, during this early period, a handful of German spies came parachuting out of the skies or arriving by boat, or even by submarine; and there were constant rumours of yet another concerted attempt to turn this latest difficulty of England's into another opportunity for Ireland (with German aid) to finish off the job and recapture the Six Counties of Northern Ireland, partitioned off by Lloyd George under pressure from the Ulster Unionists in 1921.

Papers later released reveal that in June 1940, British Intelligence informed Dublin that an IRA-supported German invasion was imminent; plans for an airborne attack on Ireland to precede an invasion of Britain had been found by Dutch officers searching a captured member of the SS during the German invasion of the Low Countries.

But de Valera did not flinch from dealing with the IRA every bit as firmly as Cosgrave had done. He had no time for the bombing campaign in Britain – 'There is no use appealing to force if it is obvious that force is not going to be effective,' he said – and introduced legislation to deal with the IRA even before the British did: on 14 June 1939, he brought in a new Offences Against the State Act which allowed for the setting up of a military tribunal, imprisonment and detention without trial. During the entire period of The Emergency, five IRA men were executed, three died on hunger strike, more than 500 were interned without trial, and thousands were arrested for questioning and held for varying periods. De Valera put his point of view across very firmly, on a number of occasions: 'We have been elected by the firm vote of the people in two elections. We are the lawful Government of this country. No other body has any right to talk to [or for] the Irish people but ourselves,' he said in February 1939, and later, when the IRA prisoners first went on hunger strike: 'The alternatives which we are forced to face are the alternatives of two evils; one to see men die that we do not want to see die, if we can save them; the other to permit them to bring the state and the community as a whole to disaster.'

But life went on: in the same week as the first hunger striker died, Aer Lingus took delivery of the first of a fleet of 21-seater Douglas DC3 Dakota 'luxury' air liners, as those spartan troop-carriers were called in those days, and throughout the war trans-Atlantic seaplanes continued to fly into the base at Foynes carrying generals, politicians, film stars and VIPs of all sorts, who frequently spent a few days in Ireland before carrying on to Southampton Water, or to Lisbon.

After Dunkirk and the fall of France, and the collapse of the German attempt to invade Britain, when Hitler transferred the attention of his panzer divisions to the Russian front, fears of a German invasion of Ireland diminished appreciably, as did the possibility of an anticipatory invasion by British forces, though pressure to allow the British Navy to regain the use of the Treaty Ports handed back to Ireland during the Munich crisis was stepped up considerably.

And although the general public knew nothing about it at the time, nor indeed for many years later, after the fall of France the British Government offered de Valera a united Ireland if he would agree to come into the war on the Allied side, but Dev turned down the offer because he didn't believe that the British would be in any position to deliver the goods; he understood the recalcitrance of the Ulster loyalists far better than the British did then, or at any time before that, or at any time since.

To go into the matter in more detail, some additional material on this period has recently come to light in *Crying in the Wilderness* (Belfast: Institute of Irish Studies, 1995), Andrew Gailey's book about Jack Sayers, editor of the *Belfast Telegraph* during the war years. Sayers was one of three officers of the Ulster Division of the RNVR who served on Churchill's personal staff during the war. The others were Sir Richard Pim, later to become Inspector-General of the RUC (Royal Ulster Constabulary), and H. W. McMullan, who became head of the BBC in Northern Ireland. Sayers knew about the deal that Churchill offered Dev (by telegram) on 8 December 1941, promising him a United Ireland if he would agree to join the Allies. Pim's unpublished memoirs, dated 21 July 1941, describe a lunch at Downing Street attended by Churchill, Lloyd George and J. M. Andrews who had just succeeded Craigavon as premier of Northern Ireland:

The three prime ministers proceeded with the assistance of wine glasses, salt and pepper pots, to discuss in detail the Irish Question since 1900. The discussion lasted over an hour ... and both Lloyd George and Mr Churchill made it clear that they regretted no step they had ever taken on the Irish Question, neither, under any circumstances, would they permit the coercion of Ulster in the future. At the same time, both made it clear that they still entertained the hope that in the future some statesman would rise in Ulster who would feel justified in making a move towards closer harmony with the South. Similarly, it was their hope that Eire would produce a statesman who would make a reciprocal move towards closer harmony with Northern Ireland. They believed that if such a change of heart was to be found in the North and in the

South, *then the North, because of the history of its ancestors* [my italics, not Pim's] *would automatically become the real controller of the new Ireland, which she would bring again fully within the folds of the British Empire.*

Such a thought might have been conceivable in 1941; these days the British know, at least as well as anybody else, that the Southern Irish, as they like to think of them, have become among the most persuasive movers and shakers of the European Union – half the authoritative voices you ever hear from Brussels have marked Irish accents – and there is no longer any way that the Southern Irish would allow themselves to be controlled by the Ulster Unionists, with or without the Tories tugging at their coat-tails.

Even when the US entered the war in December 1941, after the Japanese attack on Pearl Harbor, de Valera announced apologetically: 'We can only be a friendly neutral,' though when 240,000 GIs arrived in Northern Ireland in 1942, where they were billeted until D-Day, neutral Ireland worked out a series of secret arrangements for cooperation with the Allies, including contingency plans which incorporated the American troops based in Northern Ireland in the event of a German airborne attack on Ireland. The American ambassador to Ireland, David Gray, summed up de Valera's attitude by saying that 'he was not pro-German, not personally anti-British, only pro-de Valera.' And it was widely, if not openly, conceded that Ireland's neutrality was heavily tilted towards the Allied side. To take one example, initially the Irish Government applied the rule that if any belligerent aircraft made a landing on Irish territory, the crew would be interned for the duration. Before long, however, a distinction had been drawn between operational and non-operational flights which enabled them to find a formula under which British, and later American, planes could be released. The British usually repaid the Irish for the fuel they supplied to enable these planes to return to base.

The whole period was one of extraordinary contrasts. I knew the German Ambassador Edouard Hempel well, and was very friendly with Karlheinz Petersen, who was his press attaché and was widely believed to be a German spy; he certainly was a committed Nazi. We also went to afternoon tea-dances, of all things, with Itchi Hashi, first secretary to the Japanese Ambassador, Mr Beppu, whom I also knew fairly well as a young reporter in Dublin, and who seemed to me to be far more interested in playing golf than in spying. And needless to say, we were equally friendly with many members of the staff of the American Embassy. Also, I was first introduced to the work of the painter, John Piper, by the poet John Betjeman, who had a collection of Piper's splendid studies of blitzed churches in the office where he worked as press attaché to Sir John Maffey, the British Representative in Ireland. He was not called the British

Ambassador because that would have amounted to a recognition on Britain's part of de Valera's claim, made in his 1937 Constitution, that Ireland was now a sovereign independent nation. Interestingly, David Gray, the American Ambassador (who was married to an aunt of Franklin D. Roosevelt) although he loved Ireland was extremely unsympathetic to Ireland's neutrality, unlike Maffey, and could make neither head nor tail of de Valera.

The American troops in the North attracted train-loads of young Irish women anxious to sample the novelty of dating a Yankee GI, and possibly being presented with a pair of the new nylon stockings. And in turn, tempted by the tales of bright lights, succulent steaks and glorious Guinness, hundreds of GIs in mufti came south and rubbed shoulders in the Dublin pubs and restaurants with members of the Irish armed forces, with officers and men from the British armed forces – many of them Irish, on leave in Ireland and also in plain clothes – as well as, for all we know, with German spies and members of the IRA on active service.

Another attraction Ireland offered at this period was a very active literary and theatrical scene. R.M. Smyllie, the legendary editor of the *Irish Times*, had set up the nearest thing to a Paris left-bank café in the Palace Bar in Fleet Street, where he spent his evenings surrounded by the literati of Dublin and distinguished foreign correspondents from London, Washington and New York, drawn to Dublin not only by the abundance of good food and drink but also by the sort of literary and artistic circle with had disappeared in Paris and London on the outbreak of war. Among Smyllie's circle was a young civil servant and authority on the Irish language, Brian O'Nolan who, under the pseudonym Flann O'Brien, had written a not very successful novel in 1939 called *At Swim-Two-Birds*; it got very good reviews but was not widely read because a warehouse containing the entire edition had been destroyed in the Blitz, though it has since become a cult classic. Smyllie commissioned O'Nolan to write a humorous column in Irish and English for the *Irish Times* under the pseudonym Myles na gCopaleen.

Myles's first column speculated on possible Irish translations of such terms, then in common use in the newspapers, as Axis and Molotov cocktail; they came out as *Mol* and *brad-bhaschaod Mhalatabh*. Before long he was advancing the theory that the spelling of the Russian General Timoshenko was incorrect; it should of course be Tim O'Shenko, since he was Irish and in fact had a brother Tom O'Shenko living in Limerick. But Myles – as we all began to call him from this period on – was basically a very serious student of the Irish language and one of his objects in writing the bilingual column – the other being of course to obtain enough money to indulge his insatiable appetite for whiskey – was to demonstrate that not everything written in Irish need necessarily be dull, pious, prissy, chauvinistic twaddle, an impression painstakingly achieved by successive Irish Governments ever since the Treaty.

For the first months of the war, the Irish newspapers frequently ran stories about daring raids and sorties commanded by officers in the British Army who had come from southern Ireland, or Eire as it was then known, and the *Irish Tatler and Sketch* frequently printed photographs of parties of young Irishmen in RAF uniforms taken at air bases 'somewhere in England'; but before long the Press Censor, appointed to ensure that nothing would appear in the Irish newspapers that might conceivably imperil Ireland's neutrality, began to cut out all such references, a situation which forced Smyllie to get up to all sorts of tricks to outwit the Censor. Irish members of the British Army killed in the desert war were reported as having 'died of lead poisoning in the Libyan Desert', and one of the most celebrated instances of his ingenuity in this direction was when Johnny Robinson, a former *Irish Times* reporter, went down with the *Prince of Wales*, somewhere off Singapore. Smyllie ran a story to the effect that the many friends of Mr John A. Robinson, formerly of the *Irish Times*, would be relieved to hear that 'he is now fully recovered from a recent boating accident in the Pacific'.

Although de Valera's declaration of neutrality cut Ireland off for six years from the whole mainstream of European, even world events, and could easily have driven the almost non-existent Irish economy into the ground and enhanced the intellectual and cultural isolation assiduously achieved by the first native governments with their narrow-minded and censorious attitudes, in many ways The Emergency was a crucial watershed for the new state. The sudden realisation that we were now about to have to fend for ourselves in a world much too preoccupied with its own far graver problems to bother about any of Ireland's puny ones led to the formation of a state shipping company, Irish Shipping Ltd (of which more later) which began with the purchase of a salvaged Greek vessel abandoned by its crew during the Spanish Civil War and grew rapidly into a large and efficient fleet of merchant ships; a trebling of the amount of land under tillage; a radically new scientific and industrial approach to the processing of Ireland's only indigenous fuel, turf; even a plant capable of manufacturing paper out of native Irish straw, and numberless other ingenious innovations, all of which grew out of sheer necessity.

And the very fact that Ireland was for six years almost totally cut off from any cultural connection with the rest of the world forced the Irish intellectuals – and indeed many of the plain people of Ireland, as Myles always called them – to start thinking for themselves. What was at first contemptuously labelled 'the liberal ethic', which began with mild protests against book and film censorship and undue clerical interference in everyday life and which ended, only the other day really, in the current situation in which divorce is legal; pregnant women are entitled to obtain information telling them where (outside Ireland) they can obtain abortions; contraceptives are freely available; gays and lesbians have their own annual film festival; one-parent families are accepted everywhere as perfectly natural and normal, and the threat of a skelp of the crozier has lost all of the fearsome sting it once possessed in what must now be one of the most permissive societies in Europe . . . all this had its genesis during the dark days of The Emergency.

1

❧❧❧❧

IReLANO, SepTemBer 1939

September 1st, 1939, according to my recollection, was a brilliant autumn day, a day of Dresden china blue skies, sparkling yellow sands and transparently mauve mountains: what we always called in Ireland a pet day. But that could have been part of the magical haze that surrounded that period of my life, the shadow line, as Joseph Conrad called it, that brief space between the time when you haven't quite realised what it is all about, and the moment when you are forced to accept the fact that you know exactly what it *is* all about, and that if things haven't worked out according to your plans, there's nobody you can possibly blame except yourself.

Dublin Bay that morning was, as it so often is, breath-takingly beautiful, with a stiff breeze tearing the tops off the waves. Sturdy men marched sternly over the rippled sandscape accompanied by dogs chasing the shadows of seagulls from puddle to puddle. It was a pretty ordinary morning on Sandymount Strand.

But not for me. I had heard the early news and knew that, despite all the treaties, the promises, the guarantees, the German army that morning had invaded Poland, pushing their panzer divisions through peaceful, sleepy borderline villages, slaughtering the men, raping the women, bundling the tiresome old-age pensioners off to concentration camps. I don't know what I expected, really: perhaps to see a thin line of fighter aircraft in the sky above the Irish Sea between Holyhead and Dun Laoghaire, heading for Howth, or maybe a line of destroyers and cruisers and aircraft carriers closing in on Ireland. That would have made sense. No point in a direct attack on so well-fortified an island as Britain, but Ireland, undefended even by the remnants of the British Navy after Chamberlain returned what we used to call the Treaty Ports, was almost defenceless. The ports had been returned in 1938, at the time of the Munich crisis, as part of Chamberlain's general policy of appeasement, in an effort to heal the wounds left by the executions following the 1916 Easter Rising, the activities of the Black and Tans and the Auxiliaries during The Troubles (now known as the War of Independence) and, finally – after de Valera became Prime Minister in 1932 – the hardships caused by the Economic War.

So what I was really expecting that morning in September 1939, on Sandymount Strand, was the arrival of a task force of Germans to take over Eire as it was then known, and establish military and naval bases there in preparation for the main attack on England, whenever that might happen. My mind was full of images of fast and dangerous warplanes, exaggerated artists' concepts of which appeared regularly in an aviation magazine to which my parents subscribed on my behalf at that time. The planes on the covers of these magazines were unbelievably modern – all sleek, streamlined, low-wing monoplanes at a period when Britain was still largely dependent on the Hawker Hart and the Hawker Fury, not to mention the Fairey Swordfish – affectionately known as the string-bag – old-fashioned biplanes fundamentally not very different from the British and French fighters of the First World War, like the Sopwith Camel and the Nieuport (which I knew all about because one of my hobbies had been building model aeroplanes) and it seemed to me on that morning that if the Germans took it into their heads to choose Ireland as a base against which to commence operations against England and France, there was nothing much we could do about it except perhaps dig a few trenches, build some air-raid shelters and keep our heads well down.

It had all happened so suddenly. Only a few days earlier, the army jumping teams representing cavalry units from the French, German and British armies had been peacefully competing for the Aga Khan Trophy at the Royal Dublin Society's Horse Show in Ballsbridge. And now they were on the brink of war.

*   *   *

That September, 1939, I was aged seventeen. I had just completed my Leaving Certificate and had done very well, particularly in Irish, French and English. I had also taken the Trinity entrance exam, and one of my many ideas was to go to TCD to train for the diplomatic service. My best friend at that period was George Warnock, whose brother William – about ten years older than I was, and with qualifications similar to those I was aiming to get, was currently Chargé d'Affaires in Berlin. I didn't much fancy Berlin; I had my sights set on Paris and – because I was also passionately interested in painting – thought it might be possible to slip away from time to time from the Champs Elysées or wherever the Irish Legation was situated, and mix with the models, midinettes and mesdames of the Quartier Latin. At the same time I was well aware that my father was facing severe financial problems at that particular period since a British firm he had represented in Ireland had recently gone bankrupt, and it was beginning to look increasingly unlikely that he would be able to support me while I was at Trinity College.

My father was a veteran of the First World War. He had tried originally to join the Royal Army Medical Corps and, when unable to do so, had joined the Leinster Rifles – having successfully lied about his age – and found himself transported at the age of sixteen from a small house in Ringsend, almost on the banks of the River Dodder, to a beach on the Dardanelles. There he swam in the Hellespont in intervals between being shelled by the Turks from the heights. After Gallipoli he was transferred to Palestine and marched up the Nile to Cairo, with Allenby's army; Lawrence of Arabia was simultaneously leading the Arab army up the other bank of the Nile. From there he went back to Palestine and then to the Balkans, where he was rendered unfit for further military service by being blown off a mule by a stray piece of Turkish shrapnel.

After the war he had managed to acquire for us one of what were known as the soldiers' cottages; there were estates of them, if that's not too grand a word, all over Dublin, and ours was at Seafort Gardens, near Sandymount, a village a few miles south of Dublin on the shores of Dublin Bay, now a fashionable suburb.

For three or four days we Gray children had been on our own while our parents toured Northern Ireland with my Uncle Hugh, who then lived at Rhyl in North Wales, where he was one of the 'men from the Pru'. When war began to appear inevitable, he decided that he would like to take another look at his ancestral home in Rostrevor, near Warrenpoint, Co. Down, and had asked my father and mother to accompany him, using our family car for the purpose of the expedition. He reckoned, quite rightly, that by now the Gray children were well able to look after themselves for a week or two. It was the sight of the car, parked there in its familiar place in the front garden, that really threw me when I arrived back at the house that morning. We hadn't been expecting them for another week.

I quickly learnt that the decision to cut short their holiday had been my uncle's; he didn't want to find himself stranded in the new Irish Free State, or Eire, or whatever they called it now, cut off from all his business interests in Wales – which could easily happen, he argued, the way the IRA had been behaving recently. He had already changed his ticket in Westmoreland Street, in Dublin, while passing through the city that morning, and we all went out to Dun Laoghaire that evening to see him off on the mailboat.

When we returned, I went out into the garden and sat on the running board of the Citroën – in those days, all motor-cars had a running board that you could sit on – and looked up at the crystal-clear, starry sky. Still not a sign of a single Messerschmitt. Well, it couldn't be very long now . . .

I know now – because I have since researched and written several books on various aspects of Ireland's political history – but I don't imagine that I knew or even cared then, since in our house the wireless was almost always tuned in to the BBC, that both the Dail and Senate sat all the next day, late into that Saturday night and well into Sunday morning, the Senate until 4.45 a.m., the Dail until 5 a.m., discussing this new emergency which had befallen Ireland.

With hindsight, we all know the reason for that inordinately long session of the Irish Parliament. The situation was not quite as simple as my father's frequent statement of it, but it was very nearly so:

'History will never forgive de Valera,' he used to say, 'for splitting Sinn Fein on the Treaty and precipitating the Civil War.'

At the time, it seemed to me that the Civil War was away in the far distant past, as remote as the Boer War or the Charge of the Light Brigade; after all, I had been born during the night of the day when Michael Collins was killed in an ambush in his native County Cork, on 22 August 1922. But on that Saturday morning in September 1939, de Valera had only been in power for seven years.

Before that, he had been in opposition for about four years, and before that again had spent a couple of years in the political wilderness, living in a dream world in which the only true, legitimate Government of Ireland was the second Dail, elected in May 1921, when Sinn Fein, using the British electoral machinery set up to elect a parliament for Northern Ireland under Lloyd George's 'Better Government of Ireland' Act of 1921, was returned unopposed in every single constituency in the 26 counties apart from the four Trinity College seats. Furthermore, for a time at any rate, de Valera believed the true and legitimate army of that government to be the defeated 'irregular' Irish Republican Army, the anti-Treaty rump of the old IRA in fact.

In a way there was a mad kind of logic behind this pretence. The Irish Republic had been in a sense established as a fact by Pearse's proclamation from the General Post Office at the outbreak of the Easter 1916 Rising, though it was a fact not recognised for a moment by Britain nor by more than a small handful of Irish people. It had been reaffirmed by the first and second Dail, and so long as there were people in the country prepared to accept the Republic as a fact, even if they happened to be a defeated minority, it would remain a fact, at any rate according to de Valera's curious way of thinking. So the ghost assembly of the second Dail was merely keeping the concept of the Republic alive until the time was ripe to whip up a majority in its support. According to this school of thought, the legitimate Government of the Irish Free State was a mere junta, a puppet assembly without any authority to run a country or maintain a standing army.

All very fine in theory, but in reality there had been several elections since the one that elected the second Dail, including the 'pact' election on the Treaty in 1922, so-called because de Valera tried to con Michael Collins into an arrangement whereby both the pro-Treaty and the anti-Treaty sections of Sinn Fein would put up agreed 'panel' candidates who would go forward for election unopposed. This was a formula designed by de Valera to stave off personal defeat, though Collins quickly saw through it and repudiated the deal before the election. The pact election had resulted in the third Dail which, whether de Valera recognised it or not, had accepted the Treaty, albeit by a narrow margin of 64 to 57; and there had followed another election in 1923 which de Valera recognised at least to the extent of putting forward candidates.

In 1923, de Valera had been jailed as a dangerous outlaw. In 1926, finding the political wilderness – in which he could discover little opportunity for exercising his favourite faculty, the sound of his own voice – a boring and barren environment, he began to look around for ways and means of entering the Dail again, and let it be known that if the Oath of Allegiance to the British monarch could in some way be removed, he might well enter the Free State Dail and work with the Cosgrave Government as a constitutional opposition.

His Republican comrades were appalled at this complete change of front, which these days we would call a U-turn. How could Dev possibly enter a Parliament he had resolutely refused to recognise and work with what he had always referred to as an illegal junta, a puppet government controlled by Britain? Then in 1925 he himself was repudiated by the IRA, Sinn Fein and the ghost assembly of those surviving Republican members of the second Dail and had to start all over again from scratch with a new political party. He called this new party Fianna Fail (literally 'Soldiers of Destiny', though with heavy patriotic overtones, since the Fianna were the ancient Celtic Warriors of folklore and Inis Fail, the Island of Destiny, was one of the many legendary names for Ireland). In 1927, in spite of all that had happened, in spite of all the former comrades lost in the fighting during the Civil War and in the executions, Dev led his 'Warriors of Destiny' into the Dail and took the oath, declaring that it wasn't really an oath and that he wasn't really signing it anyway. He was probably not greatly surprised to learn that the IRA's only reaction to this was to add his name to the already long list of authorities which they refused to recognise; certainly, he was acutely aware of the effect his defection might have on those still staunchly ensconced in the Republican strait-jacket, and admitted that 'those who continue on in that organisation which we have left [Sinn Fein] can claim exactly the same continuity that we claimed up to 1925', a remark which was to cause him considerable trouble when he eventually found himself in control of the country.

Barely a month before de Valera's dramatic decision to take the Oath, the strong man of the Cosgrave Government, Minister for Justice Kevin O'Higgins, was shot dead in broad daylight as he left his home in Booterstown to go to Mass. That those responsible for his assassination were never apprehended graphically illustrates the still disturbed state of the country at that time. And as soon as de Valera entered the Dail, the IRA naturally stepped up their activities against a man they now regarded as a traitor to the cause.

After a little over four years in opposition, de Valera succeeded in winning an overall majority and formed a Government. What really brought down the Cosgrave Government was its strong-arm methods of dealing with the frequent IRA raids and reprisals which continued to plague the country. In October 1931, exasperated at the way IRA gunmen had literally been getting away with murder, because of the natural reluctance of juries to find IRA members guilty of anything, Cosgrave had set up a Military Tribunal to deal with such cases, with the power to impose the death penalty. At the same time, the IRA – along with a mixed basket of other Republican and Communist-sounding organisations like the Fianna Eireann, Saor Eire (Free Ireland), Cumann na mBhan (the Women's Branch) and the Friends of Soviet Russia – was banned and declared to be an illegal organisation.

A few days after he took office as premier, de Valera suspended the Military Tribunal and revoked the orders declaring the IRA, Saor Eire and the other banned organisations unlawful. Within a fortnight he had abolished the Oath of Allegiance to the British monarch as a meaningless relic of imperialism. He next announced that he was witholding the Annuities, the half-yearly mortgage repayments made by Ireland's (relatively) new landed gentry, the peasant proprietors, for the farms for which they had previously paid rent to absentee landlords in England. The money was paid to the Irish Government, which passed it on to the British Government, and it was used to pay off the holders of an original Government loan stock issue raised early in the century to end the Land War by buying up the land of the absentee landlords at a very favourable price. The British replied by imposing penal tariffs on imports from Ireland, and the Economic War ensued. It ended in 1938, as mentioned above, when Chamberlain – in yet another gesture of appeasement – handed back the ports to Ireland and accepted a lump sum in final settlement of the Annuities.

But despite all his efforts to woo the IRA with pensions similar to those paid to the regular army, compensations for wounds and property damage, and recruitment into a special Army Volunteer force and into a special police detachment formed to fight General O'Duffy's fascist Blueshirts, the hard core of the IRA remained as recalcitrant as ever and as bitterly opposed to de Valera's government as they ever had been to the British and Stormont ones.

In 1936, de Valera considered that the continuing IRA activities justified him in his decision to declare the IRA an unlawful organisation again and, for a period, to revive Cosgrave's Military Tribunal. And in 1939, as mentioned above, when the bombing campaign in Britain began, he reintroduced – again on a temporary basis – his measures against the IRA.

And during that all-day, all-night sitting on 2 September 1939, de Valera managed to persuade the Irish Parliament to prepare itself to bring back arrest on suspicion, internment without trial and trial by Military Tribunal without any right to appeal, but nevertheless with power to pronounce the death sentence. Reading the accounts of the debates, it doesn't seem as if he and his ministers were greatly concerned with the principal problem the war presented: how was Ireland going to exist as a neutral country in a world at war, a country with no mineral resources, no developed industries, currently not producing nearly enough grain to provide its people with their daily bread, and without even one single deep-sea cargo vessel with which to bring in essential supplies from abroad, even assuming that any were obtainable? One army officer, Captain T. McKenna, recognised the problem; he described 2 September 1939 as the day 'realisation dawned on Ireland that the country was surrounded by water, and that the sea was of vital importance to her'.

I don't for a moment imagine that any member of my family had paid the slightest attention to what was going on in the Dail and Senate all day on Saturday and well into Sunday morning, and I suppose the next thing I remember is all of us crouching around the wireless set as the time approached eleven o'clock on Sunday morning, 3 September. Through the loud hiss of radio interference to which we were all accustomed in those days, we eventually heard the cracked voice of Chamberlain telling the world that the undertaking the British Government had required from Herr Hitler (to withdraw his troops from Poland) had not been received, and that consequently Britain was 'now at war with Germany'.

I don't remember what happened next. Knowing how my father felt about de Valera, I don't suppose we listened to his broadcast to the nation that Sunday evening, announcing the Cabinet changes he had made during the long Saturday sitting which turned Frank Aiken into the Minister for the Co-ordination of Defensive Measures (which included censorship of the press), and put the practical and pragmatic

Sean Lemass in charge of Supplies, a very smart move. Aiken had previously been Minister for Defence, and in a sense his new appointment was a demotion; but de Valera knew that given half a chance, Aiken would order an attack on the Six Counties, an exercise he himself was anxious to avoid at all costs.

On Monday 4 September which, to everybody's surprise, turned out to be an emergency bank holiday, news reached us that a ship called the *Athenia* had been sunk by a torpedo from a German submarine somewhere in the Atlantic off the west coast of Ireland, and that about 450 survivors were about to be landed in Galway. We saw their pictures in the papers a couple of days later: wan, confused, puzzled people, wrapped in blankets and being helped ashore by Norwegian sailors from a vessel called the *Knut Nelson*, but it still didn't really impinge; whatever my parents may have thought, I didn't regard it in any way as our war, and it didn't occur to me that Ireland could or should become involved in it unless, as I still believed, the Germans were about to launch an attack on Ireland in preparation for an invasion of Britain.

What nobody in Ireland expected – any more, I suppose, than anybody did in England – was the so-called 'phoney' war that went on for the next six months.

2

✥✥✥✥

GROWING UP IN DUBLIN

Naturally enough, I suppose, it was during those early months of the phoney war when I was growing up that Ireland's decision to remain neutral was most often criticised, during arguments in homes and pubs, in the newspapers (particularly the English ones), and above all among Irish people living in England, as well as among what were known as the West-British in Ireland, many of whom still referred to the British Navy as 'our' navy, and the British Army as 'the' army. In view of the intensity of the feelings aroused by the decision to stay out of the war, it is perhaps worth looking at the situation more closely. Curiously enough, not all of the English newspapers were equally opposed to Irish neutrality; *The Times* of 9 September 1939 took the opinion that 'it is more than probable that Eire's neutrality is the best possible policy that Mr de Valera's government could have adopted'.

One school of thought in the UK held that Britain's own defences were probably only just about strong enough to withstand an attempted invasion, and since Eire was for all practical purposes totally undefended, to send ships, soldiers and anti-aircraft batteries to defend the 26 counties against a German invasion would have been impossible, leaving aside the fact that any British troops sent to aid in the defence of Ireland would almost certainly be subjected to guerrilla attacks by the IRA and probably by some units at least of the regular Irish army. Therefore, it was in some respects to Britain's advantage that Eire should remain neutral – always provided that Germany respected that neutrality.

On the other hand, Low of the London *Evening Standard* drew a cartoon showing a German submarine passing a coastline labelled 'Neutral Eire'. The caption was: 'No refuelling British flotillas and aircraft to protect the trade by which Britain and Eire live.' The submarine's officers were depicted drinking a toast: 'God bless Eire's neutrality – until the Führer gets there.' And Bernard Shaw argued in a statement that the ports did not belong to Ireland; they belonged to Europe, to the world, to civilisation, to the Most Holy Trinity (a reference to the theocratic phrasing of de Valera's Constitution) and were only held in trust by the government in Dublin. He further argued that the ports should be borrowed for the duration by those to whom they ultimately belonged. De Valera would not even need to consent to this loan, just as he had not consented to the Treaty, but he would share all the advantages of an Allied victory. All he would have to do was to sit tight and protest, and England would do the rest.

But let's look at the facts. In the first place, de Valera really had no choice. To decide to go to war in support of a nation which was, arguably, occupying Six Counties of the island of Ireland by force and against the wishes of the majority of the Irish people, would not only have been unthinkable to de Valera himself and to almost every other member of the Dail with the possible exception of James M. Dillon* but almost certainly it would also have brought a flood of new recruits into the already extremely militant and aggressive IRA. At that period it would not have been possible for Ireland to go into the war on the British side without (at the very least) risking a whole new flare-up of outbreaks of violence, or possibly even another civil war.

In the second place, Ireland's declaration of neutrality was a natural and obvious outcome of the separatist policy de Valera had been pursuing ever since he first appeared on the political scene. It was also a clear and unequivocal way of demonstrating to the world at large that Irish independence really did count for something. Until the moment when Ireland declared her neutrality, most people in England and quite a few in Ireland regarded

---

* Son of John Dillon, who had succeeded Redmond as leader of the Irish Nationalist Parliamentary Party at Westminster, James Dillon was now a leading light in Cosgrave's Fine Gael Party, and the most brilliant speaker in the Dail.

all the talk of Eire as an independent sovereign state as just so much window-dressing, since the country was still clearly dependent on England for almost all the manufactured articles required to carry out the business of everyday living. But if Ireland could demonstrate to the world at large that it could legally and effectively remain neutral in a war in which Britain was so deeply involved, there could no longer be any doubt about the new state's status as a free and independent nation, in full and complete charge of its own affairs. Whether it could *survive* the war as a neutral state was another matter.

In any event, and with hindsight, we now know that of all the countries involved in the Second World War, only a handful became involved of their own volition. Russia took advantage of the confusion at the time of Hitler's attack on Poland to seize part of Poland for herself and to invade Latvia, Lithuania and Estonia, but kept well clear of the main conflict until attacked by Germany, and America preserved a benign but rigid neutrality until attacked by Japan. Poland and Denmark, Norway and Belgium, Holland and Greece all found themselves caught up in the war when they were themselves invaded, and certainly Ireland would have attempted to defend herself too, had she been attacked. What she could not and would not do was declare war on Germany simply because Britain had done so; not because her sympathies were not with the Polish people and against Germany in broad general terms, but because nobody in Ireland believed that the British really cared a hoot about Poland, any more than that they had missed a night's sleep over the fate of the Czechs at the time of the Munich *débâcle*.

There is little doubt that the British defences were somewhat weakened by the lack of the Irish naval bases, though the convoy routes almost all ran north around the Irish coast. Nevertheless, these bases would have been very useful for refuelling and refitting submarines and other naval vessels, and during the darkest moments of the Battle of the Atlantic the British must have felt sorely tempted to take them over again. That they did not do so is greatly to their credit; though Irishmen, even today, find it difficult to be grateful to Britain for not doing in Ireland precisely what she claims she went to war with Germany for doing in Poland.

Throughout the war, some people in Ireland felt that by remaining neutral in a struggle in which it was becoming increasingly obvious that the Allies were fighting for civilisation against the forces of darkness, Ireland was perversely pursuing a possibly logical but clearly wrong-headed line of action. And there were many others who believed that having made the initial gesture of the declaration of neutrality, and having established once and for all time Ireland's independence from Britain, the country might well then have thrown in her lot with Britain and America, as we all now know would have happened if there had been a German attempt to invade Ireland. But the ports became less important as the war went on, the vast bulk of the Irish people never wavered in their support of the policy of neutrality, and behind the scenes there was much closer cooperation between G2 (the Irish military intelligence unit) and the various British military intelligence units than anybody realised at the time.

In an appendix to his biography of de Valera, *De Valera, Long Fellow, Long Shadow* (London: Hutchinson, 1993) Tim Pat Coogan publishes a note from Sean Leydon, secretary to Sean Lemass, listing the kinds of help given by the Irish Government to the British in relation to the actual waging of the war. Unbelievably, among many other things they included information about the roads, railways and military facilities of every kind in the 26-country area; the broadcasting of information relating to German planes and submarines in or near Ireland; permission to use the air for their planes over a specified area; abstention from protest in regard to very frequent over-flying of other parts of Eire's territory; a constant stream of information in reply to an almost daily list of questions; the placing at Britain's disposal of information gained from an elaborate coast-watching service, and the routing of German and Italian official communications through Britain. Apparently, Ireland also agreed to the use of Shannon Airport for the West African service and the trans-Atlantic services, though both of these could not fail to have been used for mainly military purposes, as well as agreeing to obscure the lighting systems in Eire to meet the requirements of the British military authorities. In

view of this document, it is impossible for anybody to argue that Ireland's neutrality was German-
orientated, and although de Valera always took a
stoutly anti-British stance in public pronouncements,
there is a revealing tale told by Frank Gallagher,
the head of the government information bureau.
Gallagher had reported to him a pro-German, anti-
British remark made by a member of Dev's cabinet,
and Dev's reply was: 'I'm glad he made that remark.
It helps to establish the balance because I'm afraid
I'm a bit inclined to think the other way.'

Since I remembered almost nothing of the day-to-day
news between the week-end when the war broke out
and the day, about a year later, when I joined the
Irish Times, I recently spent some time in the British
Museum's Newspaper Library at Colindale, reading
the Irish newspapers of the period, to remind me of
all the things I had forgotten.

I started reading around the beginning of 1939, and
read through 1939 and 1940 and on until 1945, using
the three Irish dailies and various magazines like the
Irish Tatler and Sketch, and *Dublin Opinion*.

Flying was frequently in the headlines in those
days. On 30 June 1939, Mr John Cudahy, US Minister
to Ireland, became the first paying passenger to fly
the North Atlantic route from Ireland to America,
travelling on board a Pan-Am *Yankee Clipper* flying-
boat which arrived in Foynes from Southampton at
6.05 p.m. after a flight of 2 hours 90 minutes, and
left Foynes again at 8.40 p.m. with the first air mail

from Ireland, taking about 15 hours to reach New York via Newfoundland. I also learned from the *Irish Independent* that an increasing number of Irish honeymoon couples had been flying out of Baldonnel military aerodrome to London that spring and early summer, where they caught connecting flights to the continent; the Dublin–London flight took 2½ hours and cost £5. 10s single or £7. 7s return. Another old British military airfield at Collinstown, near Swords, outside Dublin, was being transformed into a modern airport.

Air services between Ireland and England were interrupted by the outbreak of the war, but were resumed from 22 October 1939, with a single week-day return flight between Baldonnel and Liverpool operated by Aer Lingus; from 19 January 1940, all flights operated out of the new Dublin airport at Collinstown.

There were complaints that the Irish Pavilion at the World Fair in New York had no licensed restaurant facilities and, unlike most of the other pavilions, a distinct shortage of pretty Irish colleens in traditional national costumes. Replying to this criticism in the Dail, the parliamentary secretary to the Minister for Industry and Commerce explained that in view of the national weakness, the lack of licensed facilities was justified by what would have happened at the pavil-ion if there had been a bar there, and as far as the col-leens were concerned there were so many girls of all nationalities in the other pavilions that it was a relief to get into the Irish Pavilion to get away from them.

Entertainment on offer in the Dublin theatres included the singing cowboy, Gene Autry, accompanied – though not in the singing – by two of his horses; Norma Shearer in the anti-war film *Idiot's Delight*; and two visits – one in November 1940, nearly a year after the war had started – of the Kurt Jooss Ballet Company from Germany which included the violently anti-war ballet *The Green Table* in its repertoire.

At UCD, Professor Erwin Schroedinger was giving a series of public lectures on the quantum theory and wave mechanics. Many distinguished visitors from England and even France came to Ireland for the hunting season; hunting had almost completely disappeared in England and France, where the packs had been broken up for the duration and many of the best hunters requisitioned by the army. In Ireland, hunting was still flourishing and all the hunt balls – the Louth Hunt Ball in the Gresham cost 30s (£1.50) a head, including champagne and a cabaret – were crowded to capacity, while in the *Irish Tatler and Sketch*, Doreen Maloney reported that: 'On the whole, considering the war abroad, and the increased taxation, matters are not so bad as at first expected in the hunting world.'

The winter of 1939–40 was unusually severe, with a great deal of snow and frost. The Grand Canal and the ponds in the Dublin parks, including the very large pond in the Zoological Gardens, were frozen for several weeks on end and the ice was soon thick enough for the Zoo to be opened in the evenings for ice-skating. Since this was long before the days of mass winter sports, and there was no ice-skating rink in Dublin or anywhere else in Ireland, skates were hard to come by; but attics were ransacked and skates that had once belonged to mothers and fathers, aunts and uncles, even grandparents, were taken down, polished off and refurbished so that the dancing Dubliners could try waltzing on the ice to music played over an amplifier, lit by braziers blazing from the banks and fairy-lights in the trees. In such a magical atmosphere, it was hard to believe that there was a war on, and not so very far away either.

Gertrude Gaffney, a feature writer on the *Irish Independent*, was invited to inspect the Maginot Line 'as a neutral observer' and, passing through Paris on her way home, saw many young men in Royal Air Force blue sitting on the terraces of the blacked-out Paris pavement cafés. Nearer home, villages near Blessington were disappearing one by one as the Liffey hydro-electric scheme progressed and the river spread across the fields and farms below the Poulaphuca dam. The only indications of The Emergency into which we had been plunged were newspaper advertisements for black-out material – though no firm decision had been made as to whether Ireland should be blacked out or not – and DIY air-raid shelters which could be erected by any handyman in the back garden.

In the days immediately preceding the outbreak of war, trenches were being dug in the Dublin squares and parks. Indeed, I even vaguely remember pictures of men digging them. But why? For what purpose? How could trenches dug in the Dublin parks protect anybody from anything? But trenches had become part of a post-First World War mentality, and we all considered them the best possible protection from any sort of enemy aggression. After all, it was only twenty-one years since the Armistice, and we still thought in terms of trench warfare. When as a small boy I went out to play with George Warnock, we normally played soldiers, using tinhats and haversacks our fathers had brought back from the Great War, building trenches, communication trenches and dug-out headquarters in the back gardens of our parents' houses.

On the Thursday of the first week of the war, Dr Hempel, the German Ambassador in Dublin, called on Mr de Valera to assure him that Germany would respect Ireland's neutrality, provided Ireland resolutely adhered to it too. And indeed, during those early months, ships from Scandinavia and Spain bound for Ireland were constantly being stopped by German submarines whose officers examined the ships' papers and allowed them to proceed in peace once it had been clearly established that they were carrying cargoes for neutral Ireland. For example, 10,000 cases of oranges arrived unmolested in Ireland from Spain in March 1940. German aeroplane pilots were not so cautious and considerate; several Irish ships were fired on, and some were sunk in the early days of the war.

What else was happening in Dublin at that period?

Three nuns left for service as missionaries in the Philippines, a fiercely Catholic country which had been under the safe domination of Spain for 328 years and was now, since 1898, under the dangerously materialistic and godless control of the United States. The Government fixed the prices of commodities like coal, flour, grain of all kinds and petrol to stop profiteering, offered interest-free loans to farmers prepared to increase their tillage, appealed to farmers, farm labourers, market gardeners and plotholders to grow more food, and guaranteed wheat-growers an increase of over a quarter in the price of a barrel. The Rosslare–Fishguard mail-boat *St Andrew* was taken out of service and requisitioned as a hospital ship, the *Munster* and *Leinster* were taken off the B + I Dublin–Liverpool service and replaced by the *Innisfallen* from the Cork–Fishguard service, which was suspended for the duration, and the MV *Munster* was sunk on a journey from Belfast to Liverpool, though without any loss of life.

Dublin had just elected its first female Lord Mayor, and it serves to remind us how close were the events of Easter Week and the Troubles that she was Mrs Tom Clarke, widow of the ex-Fenian tobacconist whose shop in Parnell Square had been the principal centre of nationalist activity before the 1916 Easter Week Rising, and who himself had been executed after the surrender as one of the signatories to the proclamation of the Irish Republic. One of the first things Mrs Tom Clarke did on arrival in the Mansion House was to have a large portrait of Queen Victoria removed from the wall, very sensibly, and put into storage somewhere in the basement. Portraits of Victoria did little or nothing to add elegance to any surroundings, though a huge bronze monument to the lady still dominated the space in front of Leinster House, the Irish Parliament buildings. But not for long; I was there as a reporter to witness her undignified removal by crane on 22 July 1948.

It was a time of frequent Government warnings about the unfairness of hoarding food, petrol and other supplies, and hints that petrol would soon have to be rationed, despite the fact that the £2,500,000 new oil refinery at Alexandra Basin was at last ready to begin production. And the Government announced a new scheme for compulsory tillage: at least 12½ per cent of all holdings of over ten acres would have to be made available for tillage, and whole-page Government advertisements extolled the virtues of potatoes, the perfect diet, full of vitamins and easy to grow anywhere. The first efforts to persuade unemployed men to work at turf-cutting were initially a failure; in 1940, seventeen unemployed men left Clonsast Bog where they had been given board and lodgings in portakabins in the middle of nowhere, and 4s a week with not a pub within walking distance in which to spend it.

In Britain, the Home Secretary reported to Parliament that Expulsion Orders against 113 Irish people had been made between 28 July and 30 September 1939, under the Prevention of Violence (Temporary Provisions) Act, introduced to strengthen the police in their dealings with illegal organisations in England after the 1939 'mainland' bombings.

By the end of October 1939, the Irish Government was requiring non-Irish citizens who arrived in Eire from Great Britain or elsewhere to register with the Civic Guard, and hotels were obliged to report any non-nationals in residence. This order did not affect citizens from Northern Ireland, who were in every way regarded and treated as if they were citizens of Eire.

Agreement was reached between Dublin and London that Britain would take 2,000 tons of Irish butter and the whole of Ireland's exportable surplus of bacon. The six newly acquired Lysanders of the Irish Air Corps flew over Dublin at night to test the lighting at the new civic airport at Collinstown.

The city had been plunged into a largely unpremeditated and premature black-out on 3 September, but after a few days and an awful lot of motor accidents, regulations were relaxed in favour of a discreet dim-out; the idea was to provide enough street lighting to avoid unnecessary accidents but also to cowl the street-lights and black out the more garish neon signs to avoid a tell-tale glow over Dublin in the night skies, which could conceivably be held to assist belligerent aircraft to navigate. Like so many other things which seemed at the time to have been decided by the Irish Government, this had in fact been discussed with the British and an arrangement that suited the British military authorities was adopted eventually, as mentioned above.

On 27 November 1939, the Government had announced a new Irish Marine Service to include
motor torpedo-boats and armed trawlers, whose duty
it would be to ensure that Irish territorial waters were
not violated by the belligerent powers. Until then, the
only ship in service which might loosely be described
as an Irish Navy vessel was the British gun-boat
Helga, which had shelled Irish positions during the
Easter Week Rising of 1916; subsequently (after the
Treaty) commandeered, renamed the *Muirchu* (Irish
for Sea Hound) and used for day excursions around
Dublin Bay and to the Isle of Man, it eventually
became Ireland's first Sea Fisheries Protection vessel.
It was joined by another ex-British Fisheries Protection vessel, the *Fort Rannoch*, and six small torpedo
boats were ordered from England; the first arrived in
March 1940.

Around that time, I joined the LSF (Local Security
Force), later the LDF (Local Defence Force). All my
friends, like George Warnock and Jack Walsh from
the trenches and dug-outs behind Tritonville Road,
were joining up and it seemed to me the only possible
thing to do. We all signed on to a unit attached
to a small anti-aircraft battery in Ringsend Park,
about five minutes' walk away from my home and
equipped, as far as I remember, with light Swedish
Bofors anti-aircraft guns (40mm guns which fired
2lb explosive shells at the rate of about 120 per
minute). My commanding officer (also an amateur,
part-time soldier) was T.F. O'Higgins, barrister son
of Dr Tom O'Higgins of Roscrea and nephew of the

relatively recently assassinated Minister for Justice, Kevin O'Higgins. Young Tom O'Higgins – so-called to distinguish him from his father, Dr Tom, or Old Tom – was subsequently put forward as a presidential candidate by Fine Gael, in opposition to de Valera, and gave Dev a very good run for his money in 1966. My own rank was that of private, but because an anti-aircraft battery is technically classified as artillery, we privates were known as bombardiers.

My first recollection of service in the LSF was my extreme puzzlement at the fact that those in charge of this new and (I would have thought) important unit were not merely trying to turn us into soldiers by drilling us not in English, but in Irish – which few of us, and indeed few of them, understood perfectly – but, far worse, were also trying to explain the complexities of the anti-aircraft guns and range-finders which we would have to use through the medium of Irish, translated by a not very bright non-commissioned officer, working from a manual originally written in Swedish and translated, presumably by a Swede, into extremely stilted pidgin English.

When he joined the Marine Service, Patrick Campbell, another colleague of mine in the *Irish Times*, had a somewhat similar experience; he recalled orders that sounded like, 'Go meremarshawl!' and adds: 'Some of us marked time, others turned to the right, while the largest group went on standing at ease.'

The attempt to use Irish for this purpose was soon abandoned, though I don't recall that the change to English led to any marked improvement in our understanding of the intricacies of the Bofors gun and its ancillary range-finding equipment.

It has always seemed to me that our particular unit of the Irish Local Security Force constituted a far greater threat to ourselves and to one another than it ever did to the few German planes that sometimes mistakenly wandered into Irish air space, and I count myself lucky that I suffered nothing more serious than a lacerated hand when, at summer camp in Gormanston, I managed to get my hand caught between the flange of an anti-aircraft shell and the breach of the gun, and spent the remainder of my fortnight's 'active service' sweeping out the camp.

When we first joined this extraordinary reserve army, we were issued with flimsy cocoa-brown dungarees made of some sort of denim. But before long – some time in 1941 – we were issued with what amounted to regular army uniforms, slightly different in design and a good deal greener than the British Army standard khaki issue, but as substantial and warm as the British issue and presenting no particular problems apart from the desperate wear and tear on your neck occasioned by the savage ferocity of the material involved. (Dominic Behan claimed that it was the free issue of a stout pair of boots and a warm uniform that attracted many recruits from the poorer areas of Dublin to the LDF.)

Because we were in the artillery, and not the infantry, we wore (empty) bandoliers, which hung diagonally across our manly chests and were a tiresome nuisance, but it was against the rules to throw them over the sea wall, which we were often sorely tempted to do.

During the year between September 1939 and September 1940, when I wasn't serving my country by manning the anti-aircraft battery in Ringsend Park, I was attending classes at the Dublin Metropolitan School of Art, held in a building lying immediately to the left of Dail Eireann behind the National Library. There we sketched from plaster casts, always for some reason called antiques, which included the redoubtable Venus de Milo, a bust of Voltaire in extreme old age, and Donatello's David (the one in which he sports an enormously long sword and appears to be rather coyly wearing a lady's hat) and, from time to time, from real live nude models; I could never understand why the poor, shy, awkward girls who posed for us had to strip off to the buff, while the (much fewer) young men who condescended to perform the same service were permitted to wear slips. My professors were Sean Keating and Maurice MacGonagle, and I can honestly say that I learnt nothing from them except contempt for what was then known as the academic approach to art; a few years later, when I first saw paintings by Picasso, Braque, Rouault, Francis Bacon and John Piper, I realised how unimaginative their approach had been.

Because some of the senior students at the Art School were sometimes employed (as cheap or free labour; we got the occasional free sandwich and bottle of Guinness) to help the professional scene-painters to paint the flats in the theatres, and because I had always tended to hang around with people far older and wiser than myself, I frequently found myself backstage in the Dublin theatres. This was very exciting, especially when we found ourselves surrounded by actors and actresses and, particularly, the beautiful young German ballerinas from the Kurt Jooss company.

One of my first girlfriends was Phyllis Ryan, then about sixteen or seventeen, still at Alexandra College, but acting at the Abbey Theatre in the evenings. I remember going with my father to see her give a superb performance as the young servant girl in Paul Vincent Carroll's *Shadow and Substance* and finding it extremely difficult to resist boasting to him that I had spent half an hour that very afternoon necking with her in a stable behind a house in Rathmines. I must make it clear that this infatuation was entirely one-sided, on my part. Phyllis, though willing to do a bit of rehearsal with a stand-in, resolutely swore that she was head-over-heels in love with Michael MacLiammoir, a desperate waste of beauty and energy in my view.

There still seemed to be plenty of petrol around, though it was officially rationed from October 1939: 8 gallons a month for cars up to 10 HP, 12 gallons a month for cars of 10–16 HP, and a bit extra for doctors, vets, priests and commercial travellers. But somehow there always seemed to be as much as you needed in those early days of the war, and I remember the family Citroën being stopped several times when we went out for drives in the Dublin mountains during the Christmas holidays of 1939–1940; all police and army leave had been cancelled and the police and military were holding up all cars and searching them, looking for the 1,084,000 rounds of ammunition and some heavy explosives which had been stolen from the Magazine Fort on 23 December. About fifty men in thirteen lorries had managed, without much difficulty, to overpower the entire garrison (an officer, two NCOs and ten men armed with rifles and a Lewis gun) and get away with the arms.

On 4 January 1940, the Dail held an emergency session and passed yet another emergency measure; this one permitted the Government to set up detention camps within the Curragh headquarters of the regular army. 'Henceforward,' as Tim Pat Coogan put it in his book *The IRA* (London: Pall Mall, 1970) 'the IRA men knew that, if captured, they might be thrown into the Curragh and left there until the Government felt it was safe to let them out. This disturbed more people than those in the IRA.'

By the middle of January 1940, most of the ammunition had been recovered and Irish minds were preoccupied with other matters. In December – at the behest of Sean MacBride, son of Maud Gonne MacBride and Major John MacBride* – Mr Justice

* John MacBride had fought against the British in the Boer War, and had been executed for his part in the Easter Week Rising.

Gavan Duffy had granted a habeas corpus application for an IRA prisoner on the grounds that his detention under an Emergency Powers Order, made when the emergency in question was the IRA bombing campaign, was unconstitutional since that particular emergency no longer existed. The following day, de Valera was obliged to release 53 other prisoners held under the same legislation; the Emergency Powers Orders passed by de Valera in 1939 to cope with the bombing campaign in England – and since superseded by the Emergency Powers legislation passed on the outbreak of war, in which the emergency referred to was the war between the Allies and the Germans – no longer applied.

In the middle of all this uncertainty came the raid on the Magazine Fort, and on 3 January a policeman was shot dead in Cork. On 5 January de Valera brought into force an Emergency Powers (Amendment) Act which closed the loophole which Sean MacBride and Gavan Duffy had found in the law. Under this measure, prisoners found guilty under the earlier Emergency Powers Orders could be rearrested and detained under the new wartime legislation, which meant that they could therefore be held legally for the duration of The Emergency. Furthermore, unlike the earlier Emergency Powers Orders and Offences Against the State legislation, which were passed before war broke out, the new legislation was not subject to judicial review.

The President, Dr Douglas Hyde – an Irish scholar and writer and a liberal and democratic man –

had grave doubts about the legality of this latest ploy of de Valera's and refused to sign it until he had discussed it with the Council of State and it had been referred to the Supreme Court, which pronounced it constitutional on 9 February. From this point onwards,' writes Tim Pat Coogan in his biography of de Valera, *De Valera: Long Fellow, Long Shadow* (London: Hutchinson, 1993), 'de Valera showed little leniency towards the IRA. The detention camps filled up, prisoners were executed by firing squad, and in one case the English hangman Pierrepoint was brought to Ireland to execute an IRA man. The mantle, or nemesis, of the Civil War executioners had finally descended on the shoulders of Eamon de Valera.'

Towards the end of 1939, two Irishmen – Peter Barnes (22) and James Richards, also known as McCormack (23), had been found guilty of involvement in the Coventry bomb attack on 23 August in which five people were killed, fifty wounded and thousands of pounds' worth of damage done to property. Found guilty of 'murder by association' – under an old British law of 'Common Purpose' which stipulates that if two or more persons agree to commit a dangerous felony which results in a death, all of the persons involved in the conspiracy are regarded as equally guilty of the crime of murder – they had been sentenced to death, and on 23 January 1940, their appeals against the death sentence were dismissed. Feelings in Ireland ran very high, particularly since the only evidence against Barnes consisted of a receipt for a flour-bag and some suitcases used in the Coventry incident, plus a letter to a friend in the Republican movement in Dublin; he had not been in Coventry while the bomb was being manufactured, nor was he there on the day when it exploded. Every public body in Ireland, as well as the parliament and legislature, had appealed to the British Government for clemency in this issue; more than 5,000 people had attended a meeting in Dublin chaired by the Lord Mayor, Mrs Tom Clarke; and James Dulanty, the Irish High Commissioner in London, had called on British Premier Neville Chamberlain to make a special plea for clemency in this one case. But the British Home Secretary, Sir John Anderson, ruled out an appeal to the House of Lords and the two young men were hanged in Birmingham at 9 a.m. on 5 February 1940. Many firms in Dublin shut down for the day, all theatres and cinemas were closed, all sporting fixtures cancelled and flags flew at half-mast, including those on the Irish pavilion at the New York World's Fair.

Two days later, on 7 February 1940, a sixteen-year-old Dublin boy was sentenced at Liverpool Assizes to three years' detention for his part in an abortive attempt to blow up the *Queen Mary* liner in dry dock in Liverpool; his only reaction to the sentence was to say that he had no interest whatever in the proceedings of the court. His name? Brendan Behan, and he used his experiences in detention to good effect in his book, *Borstal Boy* (London: Hutchinson, 1958).

Elated by the publicity the raid on the Magazine

Fort had aroused, and convinced that the wave of sympathy caused by the execution of Barnes and MacCormack extended to their own activities, the IRA stepped up their efforts with plans for an all-out attack on the North, finalised at a meeting in the Meath Hotel in Parnell Square, Dublin, on 17 February. But by now the IRA was under such close surveillance that before any of the conspirators had realised what was happening, there was a cordon of 150 armed soldiers surrounding the hotel. The fifteen men who were arrested went on hunger strike against their treatment as ordinary criminals and not as political prisoners. In the past, Irish governments had always given in to hunger strikers, understandably perhaps in view of the fact that Terence MacSwiney's death in Brixton Jail, after a fast of 74 days, had been one of the contributory factors in changing world opinion on the subject of the Irish fight for independence. But this time de Valera allowed two men to die – D'Arcy after a fast of 51 days from 1 March to 16 April, and McNeela after a fast of 55 days from 1 March to 19 April – and on 19 April the hunger strike was called off.

De Valera was constantly reminding his former associates that there could only be one government, one army and one legislature in the country; his Minister for Justice, Gerry Boland, put it in terms they could more readily understand when he issued a warning to what he called his 'old comrades' that 'the Government was going through with this job; they weren't going to have any more of this nonsense'.

The new Minister for Supplies, Sean Lemass, speaking in Cork, claimed that the war – unlike most other ministers and Dail deputies, Lemass, an extremely pragmatic man, frequently used the word 'war' – had created opportunities as well as difficulties, and emphasised the need to develop industries to produce essential supplies during the period of The Emergency which would also meet the requirements of foreign markets after the conflict. He was only echoing what Dev himself had said as early as October 1939, when he remarked that The Emergency could be a blessing in disguise for the Irish if it forced them to find answers for problems which would never have arisen in peacetime.

In an interview with the *New York Herald Tribune*, de Valera said that the current IRA campaign to end partition was misguided and completely harmful. Even if force were successful, it would leave a part of the population embittered. Ultimately only a common love of Ireland on the part of the people both north and south of the border would make union inevitable. Interestingly, his major fear at this period was that the Germans would attempt a parachute landing in one of the nationalist areas of the Six Countries and try to set themselves up as liberators, come to assist the IRA to take over the British military installations in the North; on one occasion – reported by John Bowman in *De Valera and the Irish Question, 1917–1973* (Oxford University Press, 1989) – he told David Gray, the American Ambassador to Ireland, that if he were in charge of

German strategy he would immediately land in one of these areas and declare himself a liberator. 'If they should do that, what I could do I do not know,' he said. And indeed, when the German spies started to arrive in Ireland, the main thrust of their argument was that the IRA should stop their attacks on the de Valera Government and concentrate on Northern Ireland.

In the Dail, Lemass expressed his appreciation of the consideration shown by the British authorities in charge of controlling supplies: 'They have been most helpful to us in overcoming difficulties and have helped us out of situations which might have been very difficult – even in regard to commodities of which their own supply was not so sure.' A couple of months later Lemass went to London with Dr Ryan, the Minister for Agriculture, for trade and economic discussions, and they were met at Euston (to their surprise and chagrin) by representatives of the Dominions Office. Despite the new consititution, the declaration of neutrality, and de Valera's frequent affirmations of Ireland's inalienable, indefeasible sovereign status, Ireland was still being treated as a UK Dominion by British government officials.

Then on 22 May – eleven days after the phoney war had turned into a real one and de Valera had protested, from the remote safety of a Fianna Fail meeting in Galway, at the brutal German invasion of the Low Countries – the Civic Guard found a used parachute, some wireless transmitting machinery, some German medals of all things, and over £10,000 in used US dollars in a swastika-shaped house in Templeogue Road, Terenure, a Dublin suburb.

Another chapter in the story of The Emergency was beginning.

3

⧓⧓⧓⧓

GERMAN SPIES IN IRELAND

Wearing the uniform of an officer in the *Abwehr* and carrying a suitcase, Captain Hermann Goertz baled out of a Heinkel bomber over what the pilot took to be Co. Wicklow in the early hours of the morning of 5 May 1940, drifting slowly down towards the muddy earth of Ireland as the plane banked away and made its way back to Germany. An experienced spy, with six years' service in England, Goertz's mission was to link up with the IRA and organise them for future cooperation with the Nazi Stormtroopers in the event of a German invasion of Britain.

His parachute carried him gently down to a landfall in Co. Meath, near a place called Ballivor. In the darkness, he struggled out of his harness, bundled the parachute away into its bag and then discovered that he must have dropped a case he had been carrying when he jumped out of the plane. This had contained not only a suit of ordinary clothes into which he planned to change immediately so that he could move around freely without attracting attention but also a wireless transmitter and some Irish money; he had other money with him, but didn't realise that British currency could be freely used in Ireland. Goertz spent the best part of the next two days wandering around the area where he had landed, hiding whenever he heard anyone approaching and spending the rest of the time searching for the missing case. Eventually he gave up, rubbed some mud into his uniform to camouflage it a bit, and set off at dead of night on the third day to walk the seventy-odd miles to Glendalough, Co. Wicklow. This journey entailed swimming the Boyne en route, as he didn't want to risk making an appearance on any of the Boyne bridges wearing a German uniform, even camouflaged as it was with mud from an Irish bog. Not to mention the fact that he was carrying the bundled-up telltale parachute.

In Glendalough he planned to get in touch with the first of his contacts, a Mrs Francis Stuart, whose husband he had recently met in Berlin. Iseult Stuart was the daughter of Maud Gonne MacBride and a Frenchman she had known before meeting Major John MacBride. Maud Gonne had been the object of the poet W.B. Yeats's lifelong, towering passion – in which capacity she had inspired some of the greatest lyrical poetry written in the English language since Shakespeare – and when over the years she repeatedly and resolutely refused to marry him, he had proposed to her daughter Iseult,* then in her early twenties. Iseult also turned down Yeats and later married Francis Stuart, the novelist, a Nazi sympathiser who had left Ireland for Germany earlier in 1940, and who regularly broadcast German propaganda to Ireland during the four years of The Emergency.

Goertz stayed with Iseult Stuart in Glendalough for a short period, tentatively establishing contact with other IRA associates whose names he had been given, while she went into Dublin and bought him a suit of ordinary civilian clothes to replace those lost in the parachute-landing; the receipt for a gentleman's suit, purchased at a time when her own husband was away in Germany, was one of the pieces of evidence considered by the Special Criminal Court when she herself was tried in connection with the Goertz affair. Both Iseult Stuart and Hermann Goertz were fully aware that her house at Laragh, near Glendalough, was under surveillance by the police and the Irish Special Branch, and they kept a close watch on the roads across the mountains for approaching cars, particularly at night.

One night, after Goertz had been with her for only a few days, Iseult Stuart saw sidelights approaching and guessed that this could be the expected visit from the police. She managed to get him away in

* Iseult was thus a half-sister of Sean MacBride, who had been very prominent in the IRA in the period during and immediately after the Civil War and was still an active member when war broke out.

time, but the bed in which he had been sleeping was still warm when the Guards arrived and she was arrested. She was charged in the Special Criminal Court with 'assisting in or interfering with the apprehension of a person who had committed an offence under the Emergency Powers Acts', which was as close as the newspapers could get, under the strict censorship regulations of the period, to what had actually happened. The case was heard in camera and she was eventually acquitted of all charges, possibly because her half-brother, Sean MacBride, had by then become a highly respectable barrister who had defended many prominent politicians and was himself becoming a considerable political force in the country.*

In the meantime, Hermann Goertz had followed up another of his leads and turned up at the home of Stephen Held, a well-known Dublin businessman with German family and business connections who lived in a house shaped like a swastika on Templeogue Road, Terenure, a suburb of Dublin, though this fact was only visible from the air. I

---

* If it seems strange that a man who was known to have been prominent in the IRA at the outbreak of war should have emerged, less than a year later, as a highly respectable barrister who was fast becoming a considerable political force in the country, the explanation is that we are talking about Ireland. For one thing, the IRA was a secret society as well as an army, and nobody could say for certain that Sean MacBride had been a prominent member; for another, de Valera and almost all of his cabinet, as well as most of the opposition, had been members of the IRA at one time or another and maintained an utterly ambivalent attitude towards it for the remainder of their lives.

happen to know about it because I did a lot of flying in a light plane over the Dublin area with a friend called Norman Ashe, an Arnhem glider pilot, in the period immediately following the end of the war, and I must say it occurred to me at the time that it was a curiously expensive gesture; if the plan was to indicate its presence and its owner's sympathies to aircraft overflying Dublin, a Nazi flag pinned on the flat roof would have been quite adequate and a whole lot cheaper. Goertz had only been living there with Held for a short time before there were signs that the local guards were again becoming suspicious.

In a supplement to the *Irish Times* of 8 May 1985, published to mark the 40th anniversary of the end of the war in Europe, Mella Crowley, who was writing a book based on memoirs dictated by her father, Dr F.H. Boland,* described exactly what happened:

Goertz was only with the Helds two days when the Special Branch decided it was a suspicious house. They drove up to the house in a squad car. The Sergeant went in and said: 'Is Mr Held at home?' There was only the old mother there, and she said, 'No.' So the Gardai went away, pulled up a side street, opened an evening paper and started reading the racing page. Held was

---

* Dr Boland, who was Irish Ambassador to the Court of St James from 1950 and President of the United Nations General Assembly from 1960, was then working for the Department of External Affairs and had been put in charge of matters concerning Germany.

no fool, and when he returned with Goertz, he saw the car with the Gardai in it. So Goertz said to Held, 'You go on in. I'll just hang around here and see what happens.'

Held went in, and was immediately arrested. The Guards searched the house and found $24,000, a number of marked maps of Ireland and some medals including an Iron Cross – to which Goertz felt so strongly attached that he had insisted on taking it with him to Ireland on this ill-fated mission – along with his parachute, his German uniform and various other incriminating items. Held was charged with the same crime of interfering with the apprehension of a person who had committed an offence under the Emergency Powers Acts and was sentenced to five years' penal servitude. Goertz, it seemed, had successfully disappeared, and nothing more was heard about him for nearly two years.

Attempts by the Nazis to enlist the aid of the IRA in the coming struggle with Britain had begun long before the outbreak of war. As early as December 1938, one Oscar C. Phaus, a journalist who had worked in the States and become a founder member of the German Bund there, was approached by the *Abwehr* on his return from America and instructed to establish some links with the IRA in Ireland. At this stage, according to Tim Pat Coogan's *The IRA* (London: Pall Mall, 1970), '. . . the *Abwehr* knew little about the IRA beyond the fact that if it carried out bombing raids in England it must be a potential German ally.'

Phaus arrived in Ireland in February 1939 and made his initial approach to General Eoin O'Duffy, the former Blueshirt leader who had been bitterly opposed to the Republican element among de Valera's supporters. However, if O'Duffy did not actually put the Nazi agent in touch with the IRA, he at least made no attempt to have him arrested, and within a matter of days Phaus had established contact with the IRA hierarchy.

Phaus's principal ally in Ireland appears to have been Seamus O'Donovan, a member of the IRA Army Council, and later in the same month (after Phaus had returned to Germany) O'Donovan visited him in Hamburg with a memorandum on the IRA's policies, and full details of its arms and equipment. O'Donovan subsequently visited Germany again on a couple of occasions. There were misunderstandings and blunders on both sides, but the upshot was that the IRA never did succeed in setting up a supply route to provide themselves with arms from Germany, nor did they respond to urgent German requests to cease operations against the de Valera Government and concentrate attention instead on British military installations in Britain and Northern Ireland. One of the transmitters which the IRA had been using to keep in contact with Germany was seized in a police raid in the Dublin area on 29 December 1939, in the course of the intensive operations following the Magazine Fort Raid. During the police raid Tony D'Arcy and Paddy McNeela, both of whom died on hunger strike subsequently, were arrested.

At the time when war broke out, the IRA, not for the first time in history, appeared to be suffering from some considerable internal confusion. Sean Russell, the Chief of Staff who, in conjunction with Joe McGarrity, head of Clan na Gael in the States, had ordered the bombing campaign in 'mainland' Britain in 1939 and was consequently on the British police 'wanted' list, went to America in April of that year, promoting Stephen Hayes to be Chief of Staff in his absence. For some reason, Hayes's appointment was never ratified in the ordinary way by the Army Council, which subsequently led to a lot of trouble. Hayes, an amiable ex-footballer from Co. Wexford – over-fond, perhaps, of a drink – did not insist on regular meetings of the IRA Army Council, and there were differences of opinion as to the proper course to adopt in the various approaches to the problem of regaining Irish unity and getting the 'Brits' out of Ireland once and for all. On top of that, the IRA in Cork and Kerry had split away from the main body as well as from one another, and the IRA in the North had begun to look to Belfast rather than to Dublin for direction.

Russell was arrested on 6 June by the Detroit police, as a precautionary measure before an official visit by King George VI and Queen Elizabeth of England who were just across the border in Canada. Some seventy members of the US Congress threatened to boycott the royal visit in protest and, as a result, Russell was released on bail. He was served with an expulsion order on 10 September and went on the run, but although he contrived to evade recapture, the wartime shortage of shipping facilities prevented him from boarding a boat to Ireland.

At this stage the Germans, who were already in close contact with the IRA, intervened and succeeded in arranging a passage for Russell to Berlin via Genoa, though an attempt to put him in contact with Hermann Goertz – just about to embark on his ill-fated mission to Ireland – failed because Goertz had taken off from Fritzlar airfield in the early hours of 5 May, a short time before Russell arrived there to brief him. Russell was then enrolled in a bomb-making course at Legel Laboratory, where he was reunited with an old friend, Frank Ryan, leader of the IRA Republican Brigade in Spain who had been captured in 1938 by Italian troops, turned over to Franco's forces towards the end of the Civil War and eventually, after a great deal of IRA and Clan na Gael Irish-American pressure, handed over into German custody.

On meeting Ryan, Russell immediately agreed to take him back to Ireland on an unspecified mission sanctioned by Admiral Canaris, the German Naval Commander. A U-boat placed at their disposal sailed from Wilhelmshaven on 8 August 1940. It was a voyage almost as disastrous as that of the submarine U-20 which had carried Roger Casement on his abortive mission to Banna Strand in April 1916: on 14 August, Sean Russell died on board the U-boat, probably of a perforated ulcer, and was buried at sea with full military honours, wrapped in the Nazi flag. Ryan, not knowing what his mission in Ireland was supposed to be, returned with the submarine to Germany, where he had a stroke the following January from which he never fully recovered, though he did not die until 1944. In the early days of his illness, he was frequently visited by Iseult's husband, Francis Stuart, at that time lecturing at Berlin University among his many other activities.

Apart from Goertz, who was still at large nearly two years after disappearing from Held's house, most of the other spies sent to Ireland by the Germans (including two Irishmen, Lenihan and O'Reilly) were arrested almost the moment they set foot in Ireland. One, Karl Anderson, was picked up at Kingsbridge railway station in Dublin on 13 June 1940, one day after he had been landed in Co. Kerry. Three others – Tributh, Gaertner and Obéd – came ashore at Baltimore Bay, Co. Cork, having sailed from Brest in a yacht, the *Soizic*, rigged like a Breton fishing boat and skippered by a famous German yachtsman, Christian Nissen. Tributh and Gaertner were South African Germans and spoke little English; Obéd, an Indian, had been sent along with them as their guide and interpreter.

According to an article by Joe Carroll – 'The spies who came down in the night' – which appeared in the special supplement to the *Irish Times* of 6 May 1985, mentioned above, 'on landing, the trio strolled along the roads of West Cork, carrying their suitcases, led by the dark-skinned Obéd, who had dressed for the occasion in a bright silk Indian suit and a straw hat. They were soon picked up by the local gardai who telephoned Dublin to report that: "Two whites and a nigger have appeared from nowhere."'

Another experienced German spy, Gunther Schuetz, parachuted into Co. Wexford in March 1941 to radio back weather information and spy on Northern Ireland's war production. He had been so badly briefed that he was convinced that the IRA and the Irish army were one and the same, and that all Ireland was ready to oppose England. He used the money given to him in Amsterdam to finance his Irish mission to buy women's clothes, allegedly for his fiancée, and, according to Tim Pat Coogan:

dressed as a becoming young woman, he made his way to the home of Kathleen Brugha [widow of Cathal Brugha, who had fought in the Easter Week Rising and had been killed in the Civil War] which was a centre of underground activity. Both Mrs Brugha and her daughter Noinin were active Republicans (Noinin afterwards married Sean O'Broin, one of the leaders of the raid on the Magazine Fort at Christmas 1939) and the police were actually coming to arrest her when they found Schuetz, who was using the name Marschner.

Arrested and imprisoned in Mountjoy Jail, Schuetz made a daring escape on 28 February 1942, using a rope and a copper grappling hook he had himself made to scale the walls. As soon as he was at large, he again contacted the IRA, and arrangements were made for a boat to take him from Dingle in Co. Kerry to Germany. However, on 30 March, the day he was due to sail, the skipper of the boat, Charlie McGuinness and the three-man crew were all arrested, as was Schuetz himself, who spent the remainder of The Emergency back in jail.

Meanwhile, Goertz had been on the run since May 1940. He remained in touch with the IRA and made several attempts to escape back to Germany. Again, according to Tim Pat Coogan:

> a plan to get him away by boat from Fenit, Co. Kerry, in February 1941, was scotched when the Irish authorities picked up his IRA collaborators, and a British patrol boat waited just outside the three-mile limit. He actually got away from Brittas Bay in Co. Wicklow but his engine broke down and he had to return. He tried again in September while German planes circled overhead, but as he wrote, 'Again my boat failed. It was extremely hard on me to stand on a broad field near the sea and watch those friendly aircraft overhead.'

On 6 December 1941, Goertz was arrested when he was caught at a house in Clontarf, a Dublin suburb.

To quote Mella Crowley's version of her father's account of it in that *Irish Times* special supplement:

> The Special Branch walked into the house as poor Goertz was having breakfast, just pushing a mouthful of toast into his mouth when the Special Branch got him. He was sent to jail in Athlone. I had a certain amount of sympathy for him because I think they treated him very roughly. In the end, when the time came for him to go home, Hermann Goertz insisted that if he was deported, he'd commit suicide.

After the war, when the other captured spies were being sent back to Germany, Gerry Boland, Minister for Justice, refused to sign the deportation order for Goertz because he didn't want to have Goertz's suicide on his conscience. De Valera asked F. H. Boland, who was still in charge of the Irish side of German affairs at that period, to get in touch with Goertz through Hempel, the German Ambassador, and to try to persuade Goertz that he had nothing whatever to fear by going back to Germany.

Boland met Goertz and told him that all his colleagues had been repatriated (which was not true; his compatriots were not repatriated until after Goertz's death), that no complaints had reached Ireland about the way they were treated on their return, and furthermore that it was Ireland's duty under international law to deport him back to his own country, where he would be perfectly safe.

Goertz was picked up two days after that conversation, taken to the Aliens' Office in Dublin Castle and handed a deportation order. While the officer was entering the details of the deportation procedure in his records, Goertz took a cyanide pill and died instantly, in that back room in Dublin Castle, rather than run the risk of being handed over to the Russians.

In the same article, Mella Crowley records her father's recollections of an extraordinary coincidence concerning the last spy to be dropped on Irish territory during the war. When Roger Casement was landed at Banna Strand in Co. Kerry just before the Easter Rising of 1916, he was arrested by the Royal Irish Constabulary under a Sergeant O'Reilly, who had a son who later went to live in Germany.

About six months before the end of the war, Boland had a telephone call saying that something or somebody had been dropped by parachute in the Listowel area. By this time, of course, G2* knew all about everybody in Ireland who had any German connections, and as a matter of routine sent a couple of Guards to question O'Reilly who, as they very well knew, had been writing to his son regularly until war broke out. When the Guards arrived at the house in a squad car, O'Reilly's son, who had just been dropped by parachute from a German plane, was sitting in front of the fire. Boland reckoned that the boy was now convinced that the Germans had already lost

* Irish military intelligence.

the war, and wanted to get back to Ireland before the British arrived in Berlin. F. H. Boland remembered him as being:

> A most arrogant young man. I'm perfectly certain he told lies to the Germans; that he was prepared to sabotage the [Belfast] shipyards and so on. He hadn't the slightest intention; all he wanted to do was to get home.
>
> We arrested him and imprisoned him at Arbour Hill, but he managed to escape and had not been recaptured when the war ended. It was the only time I ever heard de Valera swear. 'Well, I'll be damned,' he said.

In all, no more than about a dozen spies were sent to Ireland from Germany during The Emergency and the fact that there were not more, and that they achieved nothing whatever, was due partly to the disarray within the ranks of the IRA following de Valera's crackdown on them under the Emergency Powers Acts (particularly following the raid on the Magazine Fort) and partly to the fact that both Hitler and Ribbentrop not only accepted Ireland's neutrality unreservedly but also felt that it was to Germany's advantage to have Ireland remain a neutral country. De Valera's strong-arm methods of dealing with the IRA had convinced Eduard Hempel, the German Ambassador, that he was serious about maintaining a very strict neutrality. Hempel passed this opinion on to Ribbentrop and managed to persuade him that to respect de Valera's policy of neutrality was the right approach for Germany. In the circumstances, the official German policy was against doing anything that would be likely to endanger Ireland's neutrality, and the dispatch of the spies mentioned above probably represented clumsy, isolated freelance attempts on the part of units of the *Abwehr* to show some initiative and make their own individual contributions to the war effort.

So, as Coogan put it, 'Churchill's fears about the possibility of an IRA-Nazi tie-up proved groundless throughout the war. Eamon de Valera had wanted his country to be neutral and neutral it stayed, in one of the greatest diplomatic feats of the Second World War.'

4

⨯⨯⨯⨯

pup leader-writer

A great deal of my own time, as well as everybody else's with whom I came in contact in 1940, was taken up with the question of arranging my entry into the profession of journalism. Initially, it wasn't precisely my chosen profession. I would have much preferred to become a painter, but painters didn't earn very much money in Dublin (or anywhere else) in those days, and in any case I really wanted to be a painter in Paris (or better still, a part-time painter basically employed in the Irish Embassy in Paris) but that was out of the question for the moment. I knew, as did everybody else in Dublin, that the nearest thing to a Paris Left-Bank café in Dublin was the Palace Bar where the editor of the *Irish Times*, R. M. Smyllie, spent his evenings surrounded by his court of painters, playwrights, poets and novelists. And the more I thought about it, the more the notion of becoming a journalist appealed to me. Writing was no problem; I had written several (very bad) plays and part of a (dreadful) novel with no bother at all, and greatly to my own satisfaction, on an old office typewriter my father had brought home when his business folded. I was quite enjoying myself at the Art School but, although my father had now started in another business, it was becoming increasingly clear that my family could do with a slight contribution to the kitty from me.

Deciding to take matters into my own hands, I sat down and wrote what I considered to be a highly professional outline of my qualifications for a job as a journalist on the *Irish Times*. I then thought it might be a good idea to type it out to show the editor of that newspaper that I could type into the bargain. The only snag was that the old office typewriter of my father's which I was using was missing a letter, and as luck would have it that was the letter 'G'. I had become quite accustomed to leaving a blank whenever I needed a 'G' and filling it in with pen afterwards, but it took some of the professional polish off the application to be unable to type out my own name without the assistance of a pen. I sent it off anyway and when, after three weeks, I had received no reply, concluded that the missing 'G' must have ruined my chances. So I arranged with one of the girls who worked as a secretary in the Art School to type a fresh application for me. I also talked her into typing out a couple of articles I had written as samples of my style. Again, there was no reply of any kind.

Then one night when I was backstage in the Gaiety Theatre painting some sets with my scruffy fellow-students from the Art School, I ran into an old school-friend from St Andrew's College with two pretty young ballerinas hanging from his arms.

'Good God, George,' he said – and I couldn't complain because that was my name while I was at school, and before I got caught up with the arty crowd and started to use my nickname Tony which seemed so much more suitable for an art student. 'What the hell are you doing here?'

I told him I was helping the scene-painters to do the flats and asked him what he was doing. 'I'm ballet critic for the *Irish Times*,' he said. 'Among other things. And at the moment I'm interviewing these two beautiful young dancers for a paragraph or two in the *Irishman's Diary*. It's a great life.'

I suddenly remembered with fury that James Petti-grew – my best friend at St Andrew's, who had spent most week-ends at our home – had been very friendly with the editor of the *Irish Times*, a former neighbour of his father's in Sligo, and that he had joined the paper straight from school. Why had I never thought of him before, when I was wasting all that time talking to other people and writing letters to the editor on the broken typewriter? James was now clearly a very dashing young man-about-town; he looked and behaved exactly like the successful Fleet Street columnist he was later to become after the war, when he ran the William Hickey column in the *Daily Express* at one period and the John Rolls page in the *Daily*

Mirror at another. He now told me that he had already joined the Fleet Air Arm and was waiting to be called up for training in Pensacola in Florida. 'Florida, of all places,' he said. 'Think of the sun. Think of the beaches. Think of the uniform, think of all those adoring, lovely, long-legged American girls.'

I told him that I had been trying to get a job in the *Irish Times* for months, that I had written several letters to the editor and even sent him some sample articles, but hadn't had a word of a reply.

'Oh, it's pointless writing to the editor,' he said. 'He never answers any letters. He's famous for never answering any letters.' I was later to discover how very true that was.

'No problem,' he said. 'I'll arrange a meeting with old Bertie tomorrow.' Typical of James, I thought. He wouldn't dare use the name Bertie in front of R. M. Smyllie or even, if it came to that, in front of his own father. But who was I to cavil at a time like this? 'Do you think you could, James?' I asked anxiously. 'I'd be most grateful if you could.' And he replied, 'Sure. No problem. Meet me in the front office of the *Irish Times* at three tomorrow, and I'll take you up straight away and introduce you to the old bugger. See you.' And off he swept, the two dancing girls in tow.

I had seen photographs of Smyllie, but nothing prepared me for the impact of the reality the following day. He was sitting at an old-fashioned roll-top desk, and had clearly just come in because he was still wearing an enormous wide-brimmed sombrero, a gaberdine raincoat and a Trinity scarf. To

say that he was larger than life would be a gro-
tesque understatement; in that tiny, cluttered office,
he looked immense. He had a round, chubby, red-
dish face, a pair of small, perfectly circular glasses
which gave him a slightly owlish, Billy-Bunterish
expression, and under his small snub nose sprouted
an untidy dark moustache from the centre of which
protruded a Sherlock Holmes pipe, firmly clenched
between his teeth.

'Well, Gray,' he said to me, when James had introduced me and then made a hasty exit, 'Pettigrew tells
me you're a literary genius.' His tone was distinctly
affable and I think I detected a friendly glint in those
narrow, quizzical eyes. 'Highest marks in the whole
country in English in the Leaving Certificate.'

For some reason which I can't even begin to explain,
even after all this time, I was completely at ease with
this man. For the first time in my life, I felt I was
being addressed as an adult, without any of the
usual, maddening condescension, by a senior and
fairly eminent member of the community. It had
certainly never happened to me at school, nor had I
ever been treated remotely like an adult by my father
or any of my numerous relations. It didn't happen
much to eighteen-year-olds in those days.

'Among the highest,' I corrected him casually. Even
that wasn't strictly speaking true. I had done rather
better than average, but no more.

'And I wouldn't necessarily take Pettigrew's word
on anything connected with literature,' I added. I
still blush when I think about it now. I don't know

whether it was merely the arrogance of extreme youth, or the fact that I felt this instant affinity with Smyllie, but that's what I said, or words to that effect.

Smyllie started to chuckle. 'You'll do,' he said. 'Have you got a typewriter?'

I told him I had, expecting to be asked to submit some articles in the course of the next few months.

'Bring it in here at nine-thirty tonight,' he said curtly.

I explained to him breathlessly that my typewriter was an old machine of my father's: a big, heavy, office-type typewriter. There was no way I could carry it into the office.

'Go home and get your parents to buy you a portable,' he said, 'and be here with it at nine-thirty tonight. Good afternoon, Mr Gray, sir.'

And that was it. I was dismissed. The question of a salary, if any, had never been mentioned. Nor indeed what the job, if any, was, nor what I was supposed to do when I arrived in the office that evening.

When I returned that night with a brand-new Empire portable typewriter, a smallish man with thick glasses wearing the dark brown uniform of an officer in the Local Security Force was seated at a desk just outside the door of Smyllie's room.

'I daresay you must be Gray,' he said in a vague, absent-minded way, like the schoolmaster he had been. 'I'm Newman, Alec Newman, Smyllie's deputy. I'll show you to your office.' And he led me through a passage beside his desk to a little cubby-hole behind Smyllie's office, with a sliding hatch through the partition between my room and Smyllie's, and the initials PGC carved deep into the oak panelling above the desk. These, I was later to learn, were the initials of a very distinguished former occupant of the cubbyhole, the Hon. Patrick Gordon Campbell, then an officer in the new Marine Service and subsequently one of the funniest men ever to appear on British television – and probably the only man who ever made a fortune out of a television commercial by failing to get the name of the product out. The product in question was butter, and Paddy always went into paroxysms when he tried to get the letter 'B' past his stutter. The initials had obviously been carved there during an idle moment while he was sitting in this cubby-hole waiting for inspiration.

I placed my typewriter on the desk, removed the lid and sat down. Smyllie had not yet arrived, and the little suite of three offices was as silent as the grave. After a few minutes I got to my feet, went to the outer office where Newman was sitting reading *The Times*, and asked him what I was supposed to do.

'You are not *supposed* to do anything, Mr Gray, sir,' Alec Newman replied with exaggerated but quite kindly courtesy. 'You are now a member of the adult world, employed on the staff of this shuddering newspaper and you are required, *required*, not supposed, to compose a pup.'

I said, 'Yes, sir' very smartly and returned to my cubby-hole, only to realise when I was sitting down in front of my new typewriter again that I ought to have asked him what he meant by a pup. I had never heard the word used, other than in its normal canine connotation. And by the time I had summoned up enough courage to go out and ask him what he meant, he had disappeared.

I wandered out of the Editorial Department and into the main corridor, utterly baffled by the whole business. I put my head around the door of the first room I came to (which I later discovered to be the subs' room) in which a great deal of very purposeful activity seemed to be taking place, which I instinctively felt would be rash to interrupt with my petty problems, then wandered further along the corridor and eventually found myself in the reporters' room, where I encountered a small, bespectacled, pleasant-looking man seated at a desk. The Chief Reporter, I later learned: a Mr John Molloy.

'Excuse me,' I said. 'I have just joined the staff of this newspaper and I have been told by Mr Newman to compose a pup. Could you please tell me, sir, what is a pup?'

'You'd better talk to Mr Newman about that,' the man said.

'Well, that's just it,' I replied. 'He was there until a few minutes ago, but now he's disappeared.'

'You'll probably find him across the road in the Palace Bar,' the man said wearily.

I drifted back to the Editorial Department, hoping that Mr Newman might have returned in the meantime, but the place was still deserted. So leaving the

Department, I walked down the wide staircase and out through the front office to Westmoreland Street, then crossed over to Fleet Street and turned into the Palace Bar – the first of a thousand such journeys I was to make in the course of the next few years.

In the front bar I asked one of the barmen if Mr Newman of the *Irish Times* was among those present. He waved in the general direction of a swing-door that led into an inner lounge. It was crowded with people; the babble of conversation had reached a festive, feverish pitch, like a New Year's Eve party, and the air was blue with tobacco smoke.

I bought myself a half-pint of plain porter, which then cost 4d in old money (exactly one-sixtieth of a £), and sat down rather diffidently beside Alec Newman.

'I'm terribly sorry to interrupt you, sir,' I said. 'But could you please tell me exactly what is a pup?'

Very patiently, Newman put down his whiskey, turned away from the man to whom he had been talking and faced me.

'As soon as you have finished your drink,' he said, 'go back to the office, and in the top left-hand drawer of my desk you will find some sheets of bastard-size typing paper, slightly larger than quarto. Take one sheet and insert it in your typewriter. Next go through all the creed copy and the evening papers and see if you can find a suitable subject – anything that strikes you as quaint or amusing or absurd or ridiculous – and, using that as a text, fill up that single sheet of paper with as many funny things you can think up on the subject you have chosen. When you come to the end of the sheet of paper, stop and take it out of the typewriter. What you will then be holding in your hand will be a pup leader.'

I hadn't the remotest idea what he meant by the creed copy, but I felt it would be chancing my luck too far to ask any more questions; anyway, it should be possible to find a subject in one of the two evening papers, the *Herald* and the *Mail*.

Before long I had come across an announcement that the British Government had just signed a contract to buy 30 million eggs from Canada. I took this item of information and played around with it a bit, speculating on just how it would be possible to buy 30 million eggs. Obviously the eggs had not yet been laid, so the contract would be for eggs that would be laid throughout the coming months by Canadian hens. Then I tried to work out how big an omelette could be made with 30 million eggs, assuming that they could be delivered in one batch; according to my calculations, the omelette would cover an area roughly the size of the Six Counties of Northern Ireland. And so on, and so forth.

While I was working away on these lines Smyllie and Newman erupted into the office, followed by a train of supplicants who had been lying in wait for Smyllie in the front office, all down the main staircase and in the shadows outside the Editorial Department.

Smyllie dealt with them all in a brusque, perfunctory manner, and there followed a bitter altercation between him and Newman on the choice of subjects for the two main leading articles. Smyllie chose an international topic and Newman was obliged to dilate, as he phrased it, on some item of local political news. Then, for about an hour or so, the silence was broken only by the angry chatter of the two typewriters. I had long since exhausted all my ideas on the notion of Britain buying 30 million eggs and had already filled the page with my thoughts on the subject, but I didn't dare to interrupt my superiors until all was still again and I could see through the hatch that Smyllie had pushed his typewriter away and was sitting back with his feet up on the desk. A copy boy called Bill Sheedy had taken their two leaders away to the printers to be set. It was safe now, I reckoned, to approach him, so I took the pup leader out of my typewriter, carried it through into his office and proffered it to him.

'And what in the name of Christ is this?' he asked.

'It's my pup, sir.'

'Mr Gray,' he thundered, 'you have not been in this business for very long.' (This rated as the understatement of the year, I reckoned.) 'Otherwise,' he went on, 'you would know that a pup leader in the *Irish Times* consists of *one*, not two, not three, but *one* single paragraph. Now kindly take that shuddering thing away out of my sight and write me a pup.'

I took the wretched thing back, scurried off into the safety and security of my little cubby-hole and retyped it again rapidly. I made no changes what-soever, but merely reformatted it as one single, full-page paragraph.

Within twenty minutes I was back at his desk. By this time he was listening to *Eine Kleine Nachtmusik* on a portable gramophone.

'Well, that's a bit more like it,' he said, taking the pup from me.

To my surprise and delight it appeared in the following day's newspaper, not a word of it altered as far as I could see.

It surprised me then, and has never ceased to surprise me since, that people seem to be prepared to print more or less everything that comes out of my typewriter – or these days, my computer – and what is more pay me, though admittedly never very much, for doing what I would really rather be doing than almost anything else in the world.

5

⚭⚭⚭

The Start of the Real War

My delight at being so abruptly and so painlessly converted from an art student into a fully fledged journalist was tempered somewhat when I heard the terms and conditions of my employment later that night. I was expected to be in the editorial office every afternoon between 3.30 and 6 o'clock. From 6 o'clock until 9.30 in the evening, I was free to go home and have a meal or go to the pictures or meet my friends, but I was required – not supposed, *required* – to be back in the office to write my pup leader and carry out a number of routine chores by 9.30 p.m. and to remain on in the office until about 4 a.m., first learning how to, and then assisting in, reading the proofs – in search of divergences from established *Irish Times* editorial style which the peasants in the subs' room, as Smyllie regarded them, might have missed. Smyllie never left the office until the city edition went to press, an event which rarely took place much before 4 o'clock in the morning, and he expected Newman and myself to remain in the office with him for company. At 4 or 4.30 a.m. we all cycled home, together for part of the way, and sometimes ended up in Smyllie's house listening to classical music and drinking whiskey until dawn.

It was a six-day week – we did not work on Saturdays because at that period the *Irish Times* didn't publish a Sunday paper, though it had done for a brief period around the time of the fall of France – and my pay was to be 38s (£1.90) a week. Extra money could be earned by contributing paragraphs for the daily column, *An Irishman's Diary*, at that time edited by Alec Newman – for which the fee was 3s 6d (17½p) per paragraph – or by writing book reviews. Not that you were paid for writing book reviews; but you were entitled to keep the book which could then be sold for one third of the marked price at Greene's in Clare Street in Dublin, or for one-half of the marked price from Gaston's of London, if you could afford the delay and the postage. Mostly we settled for a third from Greene's in cash.

I mentioned routine chores; one of these included looking up the *Irish Times* files of a quarter of a century earlier and compiling a daily column called *25 Years Ago in the Irish Times*; another involved telephoning the principal Dublin booksellers for the purpose of compiling a weekly column called *What Dublin Is Reading*. It was all as easy as falling off a log, and looking through the 1915 newspapers proved so fascinating that I acquired a taste for browsing through old newspapers which has never left me since. But for a young man of eighteen or so who had just discovered the delights of what used to be called *girls*, the hours were desperately unsociable and inconvenient.

My first afternoon stint turned out to be another baptism of fire. When I arrived at 3.30, I found Smyllie already installed behind his roll-top desk and he immediately called me into his office.

'Gray,' he said, affably enough, 'we do not wish to be disturbed. Kindly seat yourself down at Mr Newman's desk, intercept anybody who attempts to enter my office, and say that I have left strict instructions not to be disturbed in any circumstances whatsoever.'

I found all this a little puzzling because at some stage during my preliminary course of instruction in my duties during the previous evening, Alec Newman had told me that Smyllie came into the office at some stage between 3.30 and 6 o'clock every afternoon so that he could discuss matters concerning the advertising, circulation and general management of the newspaper with the front office staff, who normally went home about 5.30 or 6 o'clock.

I had been sitting at Alec Newman's desk for no more than a few moments when a stocky, burly character with a moustache and a pronounced limp lunged through the outer door and made straight for Smyllie's room. I jumped up from behind Newman's desk and rather ineffectively tried to intercept him by placing myself bang in front of Smyllie's door.

'I'm sorry, sir,' I said, 'but Mr Smyllie does not wish to be disturbed.'

'Is that so now, son?' the man said. 'Well, I've no idea who you may be, but I happen to be the advertising manager of the *Irish Times*. So will you kindly step out of my road, young man?'

Terrified as I was of this strange character, I was even more terrified of Smyllie, so I stood my ground, barring the entrance to his office like a Roman legionnaire.

'Just one second, sir,' I said, 'and I'll slip in and have a word with the editor.' Leaving the advertising manager in the outer office, fuming and muttering under his breath, I edged nervously into Smyllie's office. Although he must have heard everything that had been said over the top of the partition, Smyllie betrayed no indication that he had heard a word of what had been going on.

'Well, Gray,' he said gruffly, 'what do you want now?'

'I know you said that you didn't want to be disturbed, Mr Smyllie, sir,' I said, slipping so easily into that approved pattern of address, 'but I don't really suppose that it applies to the advertising manager of the *Irish Times*, does it, sir?'

'It *particularly* applies to the advertising manager of the *Irish Times*,' he shouted. 'Tell him to fuck off.'

I went back to the outer office wondering what on earth I was going to say to this fierce-looking man. But he had heard Smyllie's remarks over the partition, had seen the look of consternation on my face and was already on his way out. He stopped at the door, turned and smiled at me.

'It's all right, son. I heard everything he said. I'll see him across in the Palace Bar later.' I must still have looked terrified because he again smiled warmly and said, 'Don't worry, son, you'll soon get used to our ways. What did you say your name was?'

And when I told him, he said, 'When you've finished your stint in here, come over to the Palace Bar and I'll buy you a drink.'

I learned later that this was the famous Pussy O'Mahony, remembered today – if he is remembered at all – only as the father of the popular television comedian, Dave Allen. However, for the record, G.J.C. Tynan O'Mahony was extremely well-known in Dublin in his own lifetime as a brilliant raconteur, a highly entertaining pub companion and a warm and utterly likeable member of the human race. He had an artificial leg, and we always understood that he had lost it during The Troubles. This was probably true, though I heard from someone in the Palace Bar crowd later that he had been in the Black and Tans and had lost the leg not in the course of any military engagement, but by managing to get it caught in the lift in Clery's during the period of The Troubles. Whether or not that is true, it doesn't change the fact that Pussy O'Mahony was a marvellous personality, as civil and pleasant to people on the bottom rung of the ladder as he was to those on the upper rungs, and always hilariously funny. A great deal of Dave Allen's skill as a raconteur must have stemmed directly from Pussy's genes.

What else had been happening during those long months in 1939 and 1940 when I had been busy painting flats back-stage in the Dublin theatres, making sketches of the plaster casts and the nude models in the Art School, chasing girls and trying to get into journalism?

The phoney war had ended abruptly in the spring of 1940 and the real war had started in earnest. In April 1940, Germany invaded Norway and Denmark and British troops were landed in Norway. In May, Germany invaded Belgium, Holland and Luxembourg, and Churchill took over from Chamberlain and formed a National Government. Between 27 May and 4 June, 200,000 troops of the British Expeditionary Force, along with 140,000 French troops, were evacuated from the beaches of Dunkirk and brought back safely to England. On 10 June, Italy declared war on Britain and France, and on 14 June the German Army entered Paris. A week later, despite an agreement never to sign a separate peace, France – now under Marshal Pétain – signed an armistice with Germany which allowed the Germans to occupy more than half of all French territory, including the entire Atlantic coastline from Biarritz to the Belgian frontier and all of France, roughly speaking, north of the Loire.

By August, the Germans were ready for the assault

on Britain; there were rumours that fleets of barges had been seen moored in channel ports like Boulogne and Calais, ready for the invasion as soon as Britain's air defences could be softened up a bit. Goering was convinced that the Luftwaffe could eliminate the RAF south of a line from Chelmsford to Gloucester in four days; in fact it took them one month – from 12 August to 15 September – to discover that they could never get the better of the RAF. The Battle of Britain was at its height on 11 August, and on 23 August the first all-night raid on London marked the beginning of the Blitz.

All we knew about it at the time were headlines like 150 PLANES ENGAGED IN BIGGEST AIR FIGHT YET OVER CHANNEL: GERMANS MASSING AT CHANNEL PORTS: ASSAULT ON ENGLAND IMMINENT: 14-HOUR BATTLE OVER CHANNEL: 400 GERMAN PLANES ATTACK BRITAIN.

There were isolated reports, too, on the Blitz; the damage to the Houses of Parliament and Buckingham Palace, and the raids on the London docks, and occasional pictures of devastated housing estates in suburbs like Croydon, or shots of burnt-out London buses and taxis. On 8 October, in the House of Commons, Churchill revealed the hard facts: 8,500 had been killed in the Blitz so far, and 13,000 injured. In the following month alone, November, the death toll from the Blitz was 4,558.

Inevitably, there were repercussions in Ireland. In August the Government Information Bureau issued a warning to Irish citizens to stay in Ireland because of the 'intensification of hostilities', one of the few official references to the fact that there were hostilities going on anywhere, and by September the first of thousands of Irish refugees fleeing from the Blitz began to arrive in Ireland.

The recruiting drive for the armed forces was stepped up. A recruiting film, *Step Together!* made for the Department of Defence, was shown in all cinemas; there were full-page advertisements urging 'Your Country Needs You' in all the newspapers, sponsored by firms like Aspro, Boland's Bakery, Blackrock Hosiery, Bradmola, Dunlop, Players and Wills; and a huge recruiting rally was held in College Green at which Eamon de Valera and William Cosgrave stood together on the same platform with members of all the other political parties; it was the first time such a thing had happened since the start of the Civil War in 1922.

New recruits to the armed forces, including the part-time LSF, numbered 130,000 by July 1940, even before the *Step Together!* film was screened, and by October de Valera was talking of having a reserve army (the Local Security Force) of 100,000, fully armed and with troops trained by spring 1941. By the end of July, all privately owned sporting guns had been requisitioned as temporary arms for the LSF and in October, de Valera and several of his Ministers were entertained to lunch after the salute at the end of a session of LSF manoeuvres at Howth Demense. The LSF (and later the LDF) were authorised to commandeer all motor transport, including the Mercedes cars of the Government ministers, in the event of a 'real emergency'.

I have already referred to the fact that when I arrived in the *Irish Times* Editorial Department that first evening, I found Alec Newman wearing the uniform of an officer of the Local Security Force. I soon discovered that the *Irish Times*, in common with most comparable commercial undertakings in Dublin in those days, was quite heavily involved in the matter of Ireland's defence in the event of an invasion from any quarter.

Alec Newman had been an officer in the Signals Corps of the Local Security Force even before the war broke out. George Hetherington – who then worked for Hely's, the Dublin printing firm, and was later to become managing director of the *Irish Times* – was a company commander of the LSF at Raheny, Co. Dublin, and Captain Lauriston Arnott (later Sir Lauriston, and managing director of the *Irish Times*) was LSF company commander at Howth, where he lived. He had served in the 3rd Battalion Irish Rifles during the First World War, and had been twice wounded.

George Hetherington once told me that he remembered Laurie – as we all called him, though never to his face – taking a course with him in Portobello Barracks and being put though his paces as an LSF infantryman by officers from the regular Irish army. Among his comrades-in-arms was Frank Saurin, one of the Curragh mutineers who subsequently worked as an intelligence officer under Michael Collins. Saurin once asked Laurie how he reconciled his career as an officer in the British Army during the First World War, and as a director of the West-British *Irish Times*, with his present role as an officer in the LSF of the Irish Free State.

'Well, you know,' Laurie answered, 'I always think of it like this. My house, out there in Shearwater, in Howth, that's my home. Well, if I saw a British Tommy walking across my meadows, out there in Shearwater, I'd simply have to shoot the bugger, wouldn't I?'

A future Taoiseach of Ireland, Garret FitzGerald, joined the LDF at the age of sixteen. He describes his experiences in his autobiography, *All in a Life* (Gill & Macmillan, 1991):

Advised by Fergus [his elder brother] that by joining a signals battalion, I would learn Morse code, which would be useful to me later in life – it never was – and preferring sedentary to ambulant service (I have always disliked standing), I went to the recruitment sergeant of the 6th Communications Battalion in Parnell Square . . .

The LDF was a broadening experience. I had never been much exposed to four-letter words before, certainly not at home and not at school, and it was something of a cultural shock to have to disentangle and make sense of the words that occasionally intervened between these expletives.

Going to Gormanston training camp in summer

involved a further educational process. Our captain assembled us before we left and delivered a talk so guarded that I and my sergeant, Padraic Mulcahy (a son of my father's former colleague in government, General Richard Mulcahy, soon to succeed W.T. Cosgrave as leader of Fine Gael), were totally mystified. One allusion in his speech seemed to suggest that a health risk attached to cows, which presumably, we would come across in rural Gormanston; but having had experience of cows as a child I found this unconvincing. Later on, when I learnt of the existence of VD, I realised what the enigmatic health warning had been about; and indeed at Gormanston there were a number of female camp-followers.

Then there was the Hon. Patrick Gordon Campbell, one of my immediate predecessors in the cubbyhole behind Smyllie's office as junior leader-writer. He was now, I was told, an officer in the new Marine Service. I'd heard several descriptions of Paddy from members of the *Irish Times* staff; the Sports Editor, Paul MacWeeney, a good friend of Paddy's, described him as being at least nine feet tall and added: 'And while some people have eyes that are pretty close together, Paddy hasn't. He just has this one, enormous, glowering great eye, bang in the middle of his forehead.'

But, as with Smyllie himself, nothing I had heard prepared me for the reality which arrived one evening shortly after I had joined the paper, when Paddy dropped in to give Smyllie and Alec a first sight of his new uniform. He turned out to be an enormously tall, lean, ginger-haired and already-balding gentleman, not exactly with one eye in the middle of his forehead (though I could see what Paul had been getting at) and wearing that ridiculous uniform with a red pom-pom on the top of the navy blue beret over what otherwise looked like a Victorian sailor suit. It was a compromise, the government hand-outs had said, between the British and French naval uniforms.

Smyllie asked Paddy how he was getting on.

'N-n-not ah-ah-very well, M-M-Mr Smyllie, sir,' he said firmly, or as firmly as he could with that terrible stutter.

'Why not?' Smyllie inquired, 'what's the trouble?'

'I c-c-can never f-f-fucking shout F-F-fire until it's far too fu-fu-fucking late. B-b-but I always say: "N-n-never mind, lads, let's g-g-get the b-buggers on the way back."'

6

❀❀❀❀

ᎠᎾᎷᎬᏚᎢᏆᏟ ᎪᎲᎲᎪᏆᎡᏚ

As early as May 1940, de Valera had announced a
National Defence Council, representing all the main
parties in the Dail, to safeguard the state against
all danger, and in July regional and county com-
missioners were appointed to take over the functions
of government, operating from 'safe houses' which
had been found for them in the event of Dublin or
any other vital administrative areas being cut off by
belligerent action. And on 16 July a Special Order,
under the Emergency Powers Acts, provided for an
alternative government in the event of just such
an emergency. The High School in Harcourt Street,
Dublin, was handed over to the St John Ambulance
Brigade as a first-aid post in August, and air-raid
shelters were being built like mad.

After a mysterious shooting in Rathgar, a suburb of
Dublin, one detective officer was killed and another

died in hospital later, and two men were arrested, tried by Military Tribunal and sentenced to be shot within 48 hours. It is typical of the attitude of the Government to the IRA at this period that when the two men were in fact executed on 6 September, the event was recorded only in a down-page one-inch account on a minor inside news page in the *Irish Independent*. The Irish Government was prepared to create a huge international fuss about the execution of Barnes and MacCormack by the British, but was not all that keen on publicising its own executions. Of course it is impossible to know, at this remove, whether the decision to treat the two executions in this way was one taken by the editor of the *Irish Independent*, or on the part of the censor. According to Tim Pat Coogan, all protests about executions carried out by the Irish Government were heavily censored and all that was allowed was a down-page, single column announcement that the executions had taken place.

In May also, Britain banned travel to and from Ireland without special permits, and travel between Eire and Northern Ireland without a special permit was banned from 1 July: permit offices were set up in Dublin to issue the necessary paperwork. In June, a US liner arrived in Galway to take American nationals home from Britain and Eire, and later in the year a Japanese liner, the *Husimi Maru*, en route from Lisbon to Tokyo, dropped anchor in Galway Bay to embark 170 Japanese neutrals from Great Britain and Ireland who wished to return to Japan.

In July, de Valera reaffirmed the Government's resolution to remain neutral. Thomas MacCurtain – son of a Lord Mayor of Cork murdered by the British forces during The Troubles – who himself had been sentenced to death for the murder of a detective-officer in Cork in January 1940, had his appeal against the death sentence imposed on him on 3 July turned down and commuted to one of penal servitude for life.

In August, the Irish vessel the SS *Kerry Head* was attacked by German aircraft: William Warnock the Irish Chargé d'Affaires in Berlin was instructed to lodge a protest and claim compensation.

Then on 26 August, bombs from a German plane killed three girls working in a carpet factory in Campile, Co. Wexford, two of them sisters: the German News Agency announced that Germany would express its regrets to the Government of Ireland for erroneously dropping bombs on Irish territory and acknowledged its willingness to pay compensation. More bombs were dropped off the coast of Louth and Meath in October; another Irish ship, the MV *Edenvale*, was fired on by a German aircraft off Helvick Head, Co. Waterford, in October when high explosives were dropped on a village in the Vale of Clara in Co. Wicklow. Finally, just before Christmas 1940, bombs fell on Sandycove, near Dun Laoghaire, Co. Dublin, injuring three people, and two people were injured when the mail-boat *Cambria* was bombed and machine-gunned forty minutes after leaving Dun Laoghaire.

These events happened at the height of the Blitz on Britain, and would hardly rate a reference in view of the horrific casualties on the other side, except that Ireland was a neutral country.

Bombs continued to fall on neutral Ireland well into the new year, 1941, in Meath, Carlow, Kildare, Wicklow and Dublin. Three women were killed and two men injured when a bomb demolished a house at Knockroe, Co. Carlow on 2 January; in Dublin, two houses were demolished in Laverna Grove and Rathdown Park on the same day, and the next day, bombs fell on the North Circular Road, Dublin, destroying two houses, injuring twenty people and damaging the synagogue. In his biography of de Valera (*De Valera: Long Fellow, Long Shadow*. London: Hutchinson, 1993) Tim Pat Coogan suggests that these apparently random bombings were closely related to political developments. Whenever Roosevelt warned against the dangers inherent in Ireland's neutrality in the face of German aggression, he suggests, bombs fell, causing loss of life: 'The message was clear,' he comments, 'the alternative to neutrality would be more of the same.' Well, maybe, but one would have thought a nation as ruthless as the Germans would have put across their message – if that is what it really was – a bit more forcefully than by the destruction of a carpet factory in Campile, Co. Wexford.

Earlier, de Valera had succeeded in setting up an Institute for Advanced Studies, a by-product of the combined effects of his own interest in higher mathematics and Irish language and literature and the fortuitous presence in Ireland at that period – as a refugee, interrupted by the outbreak of war while en route for the United States – of Einstein's successor in the field of quantum physics, Dr Erwin Schroedinger, who with the Rev. Patrick Browne of Maynooth Seminary was appointed to the Council of the Institute in October.

All Abbey Theatre records were broken on 5 October, as George Shiels's play *The Rugged Path* – a dreary peasant comedy of exactly the sort which had led to the break-up between the original founders of the national theatre – was crowded to capacity at the end of its tenth week; plays in the Abbey Theatre in those days rarely ran for more than a week, or two at the most; and on 15 October, the first column by Myles na gCopaleen (Brian O'Nolan aka Flann O'Brien) appeared in the *Irish Times.*

Again there was a degree of personal involvement here, and because Flann O'Brien has since become a world cult figure, the story of how a young civil servant who was also a novelist and a Gaelic scholar came to write a humorous column for the *Irish Times* might be of general interest.

Brian O'Nolan was one of a circle of lively and highly talented students at University College, Dublin, in the early 1930s. His fellow-students included Denis Devlin, afterwards Irish Ambassador to Italy; Donagh MacDonagh, son of the executed signatory to the Easter Proclamation of 1916 the poet Thomas MacDonagh, and later a considerable poet and playwright himself, and always, unfairly I thought, known in Dublin as 'the national orphan'; and Niall Sheridan, a journalist who – like another member of the group, Niall Montgomery – was an expert on Joyce and Beckett.

Towards the end of 1939, after the publication of *At Swim-Two-Birds* under the pen-name of Flann O'Brien, Brian O'Nolan and his friends started up a whole series of bogus controversies in the correspondence columns of the *Irish Times*, using several different names and attacking a number of established literary figures. One of these concerned a play by Frank O'Connor which had been produced at the Abbey Theatre, and among the letters was a bogus one from Brian O'Nolan signed 'Francis O'Connor', denouncing his namesake.

But the controversy which brought matters to a head concerned a production at the Gate Theatre, Dublin of a play by a relatively unknown playwright called Hazel Ellis. Brian O'Nolan, writing under the pseudonym of Hazel Ellis – and in those days of fairly universal honesty, nobody checked on the letters to the *Irish Times* to see whether they were genuine – aimed a devastating broadside on Michael MacLiammoir and Hilton Edwards, who had produced the play. The real Hazel Ellis rushed into print with a disclaimer, explaining that she was an ardent admirer of Messrs Edwards and MacLiammoir, whereupon Brian O'Nolan immediately replied (again using the name Hazel Ellis) denouncing this lady as 'an obvious impostor'.

This controversy was at its height when I joined the newspaper in September 1940, and at that time

Alec Newman was editing the 'Letters to the Editor' column, and encouraging Myles in his latest hoax. Alec had been a bit of a practical joker himself when he was editor of the Dublin University magazine, *TCD*. On one occasion, he had read a paper to the university's Classical Society on a little-known Greek poet, Timocrates of Cos. The point was that Timocrates was a complete invention, and Alec derived enormous amusement out of the embarrassment of subsequent speakers, who could not very well reveal that they were altogether ignorant of the great man's work but naturally could not think of anything intelligent to say about him.

When the truth about Brian O'Nolan being the writer of so many bogus letters under such a wide variety of pseudonyms came out, Smyllie became extremely nervous and for weeks seemed highly suspicious of every letter that Alec published in the correspondence columns. He would frequently pounce on a letter as he was reading the proofs and bawl out: 'Mr Newman, sir. I fancy I detect the fine old Italian hand of your friend O'Nolan here.'

Newman would normally deny the charge – though it was usually true, as we were all very well aware – until eventually one evening in late September or early October, Smyllie made an announcement, as he used to put it, *ex cathedra*: 'Mr Newman, sir, I have just solved a problem which has been vexing me greatly over the past few months. I have decided to employ your friend O'Nolan as a columnist. If we pay the bugger to contribute to this shuddering newspaper, he may no longer feel tempted to contribute gratis, under various inscrutable pseudonyms, to the correspondence columns.'

And a few days later he handed me some pages of copy, most of it in Irish, typewritten on the ruled foolscap paper supplied by the Department of Local Government and Public Health for the use of its employees, of which Brian O'Nolan was one.

'You studied Irish at school, Gray,' Smyllie said. 'Kindly read this material and assure me that it contains nothing that is scurrilous, obscene, libellous, or likely in any way to prove offensive to the management of this newspaper.'

I did so and gave Smyllie an assurance to that effect.

'All right, then, send it out for setting.'

'What about a by-line?' I asked. 'It's got a title "An Cruiskeen Lawn", but he hasn't signed it.'

'Well, obviously he hasn't,' Smyllie said. 'He works for the Civil Service. What's the Irish for badger?'

I told him: 'Broc'. And the first Myles na gCopaleen column appeared over the signature 'An Broc'.

A few days later a second column arrived in the office, accompanied by its creator, a small, shy, taciturn creature with teeth like a rabbit and a greasy felt hat. The new column had an introduction in English and then lapsed into Irish: it had the same headline but a new by-line. It was now signed 'Myles na gCopaleen'.

'I didn't much like that badger notion,' he growled.

'But why Myles na gCopaleen?' asked Smyllie.

'A Cruiskeen Lawn is a jug full of porter, and Myles na gCopaleen, as you bloody well know, Smyllie, is the archetypal stage Irishman in Boucicault's *Colleen Bawn*.'

'So?' Smyllie asked.

'I don't try to explain my jokes, Smyllie,' he said, 'any more than Picasso tries to explain his pictures. Do you know what Picasso said to an old lady who asked him what one of his pictures meant. *Madame, on ne parle pas au pilot*. Don't ask the driver. Good day to you, Mr Smyllie, sir.' And he was away.

The column was an immediate and sensational success and led to the first substantial increase in circulation that the *Irish Times* had enjoyed in years.

About the same time as the first Myles na gCopaleen column appeared in the *Irish Times*, a new literary magazine, *The Bell*, edited by Sean O'Faolain – novelist, historian and polemicist – was published. This had been a much-heralded and long-awaited event in literary Dublin, and I was completely taken aback when Smyllie called me in and handed me a copy of the new magazine, which had made a pre-publication pledge to stand firm against intellectual insularity and to assist in the maturing process still so badly needed in the raw young state.

'Tell us what you think of that in half a column,' he said.

'You mean, for the paper?'

'Of course, for the paper. What else would you write it for?'

'But this is the first issue of *The Bell* magazine,' I said.

'I'm perfectly well aware of what it is.'

I glanced down at the magazine in my hands. A list of contributors on the cover included Frank O'Connor; Jack B. Yeats, the painter brother of William B., the poet; Elizabeth Bowen; Maurice Walsh; Lennox Robinson; Brinsley McNamara and Brian O'Nolan himself. Dumbstruck at the sight of all these great names, I put it to Smyllie that Sean O'Faolain, the editor of the magazine, might well be insulted if someone as raw and inexperienced as myself, a mere schoolboy in fact, were allowed to review the first issue of *The Bell*, and I suggested that it might be far better if Smyllie wrote a piece about it himself.

Smyllie grinned at me and said, 'If this magazine survives for a decade, Mr Gray, sir, which I very much doubt, it will be your generation and not mine who will be reading it. Now go ahead and tell us what you think of it.'

Is it any wonder we all loved him? You would lay down your life for a character like that.

In October, introducing a new Electricity Bill to provide an additional £4,000,000 for the Electricity Supply Board to enable it to meet its requirements for new works and plants, Mr Sean MacEntee, Minister for Industry and Commerce, told the Dail that this figure included £800,000 for the provision of an experimental turf-burning power station to be built at Portarlington on the Clonsast Bog. This was the first big step in the mechanisation of turf production and, even more important, in the production of electricity from turf dust. At the same session of Parliament, the Government issued an Order under the Emergency Powers Acts which made it illegal for employers to impede recruiting for the Local Security Force, which had been going on in a very big way, and de Valera told an LSF parade at Blackrock that the force might well be needed after the war 'if the same spirit that animated the last peace terms were manifested in the next treaty'.

Arrangements were being made with the British Government, it was announced, to facilitate the evacuation of Irish mothers and children from areas of Britain where there was heavy bombing, and the President of the Dublin Chamber of Commerce, a Mr A. A. Brunker, told a meeting of the Chamber that despite unemployment and other problems, life in Eire was probably happier than in any other country in the old world at the present time.

In the Commons, in November, Churchill said that the fact that Britain was prevented from using the south and west coast ports of Ireland for refuelling her flotillas and aircraft was a heavy and grievous burden that should not have been placed upon her shoulders. Replying to Churchill's speech a few days later, de Valera told the Dail that there could be no question of handing over the ports so long as Eire remained neutral, and no question of leasing them. Any attempt to bring pressure would only lead to bloodshed. Later, in an interview with the United

Press, he said that if he could do anything to relieve the sufferings of the British people he would do it, but if Ireland handed over the ports to Britain for the duration of the war, it would involve itself directly in the war with all its consequences.

Towards the end of November 1940, restrictions on travel between Eire and Great Britain were relaxed: the Irish in Ireland were allowed one visit per six months to relatives in Great Britain and Northern Ireland, and the Irish in Britain were allowed to visit relatives at home in Ireland every six months, though permits were still required.

Because Ireland had been selling all her surplus agricultural products to Britain at greatly enhanced prices, and because it was almost impossible to import any consumer goods or expensive luxuries from abroad, the Irish trade balance was discovered to be in credit for the first time since the state was founded in 1922: a tiny credit balance of £45,641 was registered on 1 October 1940, but it was regarded as an economic miracle after years of adverse trade balances, years when the major contribution to the state's coffers consisted of import duties, excise and other taxes on almost every kind of manufactured article, from a corkscrew to a combined reaper and harvester or an electricity power plant.

Lord Craigavon, Northern Ireland Premier for the first twenty years of the statelet's existence, died at his home near Belfast on 24 November, aged 69, and was succeeded as leader of the Ulster Unionist party by J. M. Andrews on 13 December.

The Dail learned in November that the defence forces were going to cost £6,454,601 for the current financial year, and at the end of the year the Department of Defence announced that the LSF was to be divided into two sections, one to be taken over by the police for ARP, security fire-watch and other domestic activities, and the other to be taken over completely by the regular army from 1 January 1941 and given a new name, the Local Defence Force (LDF).

7

❧❧❧❧

BOMBS ON BELFAST AND DUBLIN

If it seems strange that the city of Belfast was not better prepared for the air raids when they eventually came, there were several reasons for this. On the face of it, Belfast was an obvious target. Harland and Wolff were one of the largest shipbuilding yards in the world: the ill-fated *Titanic* had been launched into the Lagan and, more recently, so had the battle-cruiser *HMS Belfast* as well as *HMS Formidable*.

As early as 1936, Belfast had been chosen as one of the principal centres of aircraft production for the war that was clearly coming; Harland and Wolff were amalgamated with the aircraft builders, Short Brothers, to form Short Brothers and Harland, a firm which eventually employed 20,000 people turning out aircraft like the Stirling long-range bomber and the Short Sunderland flying boat. Ship production continued, of course, and during the war the yards built or converted over 3,000 naval vessels, launched over half a million tons of merchant shipping and manufactured tanks, gun mountings, aircraft parts and other ordnance pieces. The Springfield Road factory of James Mackie & Sons, had been re-equipped in 1938 with modern American machinery; during the war this plant became the United Kingdom's principal supplier of Bofors anti-aircraft shells. Clearly Belfast as an industrial base was an important ingredient in the British war effort, a fact which would make it an obvious target for attention from the *Luftwaffe*.

However, although Belfast is not a great deal further away from the north coast of France than Liverpool or the Clyde, which had both been bombed several times, its citizens stuck to the firm belief that German bombers would not risk flying the thousand-odd miles from their bases in Northern France, which would entail crossing the British mainland twice. This view seemed to have been shared by the authorities because Belfast, a city with one of the highest densities of population in the United Kingdom, had the lowest proportion of air-raid shelters of any city of comparable size – until 1941, only 200 public and 4,000 private shelters had been built – and only half the anti-aircraft cover estimated as required for an industrial city of 415,000 inhabitants. In addition, there were no searchlights, and no night fighters available to defend the city against bombers.

There was another reason for the city's failure to prepare adequately for air raids. As well as believing that the distance between the North of France and Belfast was so great that the German pilots would be afraid of running out of fuel on the return journey, there was also a widespread belief in Northern Ireland that de Valera's declaration of neutrality, combined with his territorial claims on the whole island of Ireland, would deter the Germans from attacking them. They reckoned that Hitler would not want to risk endangering Eire's neutrality by a blitz on a city which de Valera regarded as part of his territory, even if they themselves did not accept this, an interesting example of the kind of Ulster double-think that is still bedevilling any attempt to make deals with the Unionists.

A few random bombs had fallen on Northern Ireland, as they had on Eire, in the preceding six months, probably as a result of planes becoming detached from major raids over the Clyde and cities in the north-west of England and jettisoning their unused bombs before the long flight back to France.

The first raid on Belfast took place on the night of 7–8 April, and was carried out by six Heinkel 111 bombers flying at a height of 7,000 feet, well above the barrage balloons. Initially they dropped flares to illuminate the area, and followed this up by dropping incendiaries, high-explosive bombs and parachute bombs. A great many fires were caused in residential areas close to the docks, but the casualties were not great: 13 killed, including two members of the Auxiliary Fire Service, 23 seriously injured and 58 slightly injured.

The bombing was fairly accurate, the majority of the bombs falling on the shipyards and the docks. One parachute bomb landed on the roof of the fuselage factory of Harland and Wolff's and totally destroyed a 4½-acre site used for the manufacture of fuselages for the Stirling bombers. With some difficulty, the RAF succeeded in getting four Hurricanes from Aldergrove into the air, but only one managed to catch up with the raiders and it was claimed that one of the Heinkel bombers was shot down.

Small as it was, that raid brought large numbers of volunteers into the Women's Voluntary Service, the Auxiliary Fire Service and the Civil Defence Corps. Britain sent an anti-aircraft battery and some searchlight units to Northern Ireland and there were evacuations of women and children, both to country districts in Northern Ireland and over the border into Eire. But the province soon settled down to normality, and hardly anybody who attended an Easter Tuesday football match at Windsor Park on 15 April noticed a lone Junkers 107 reconnaissance plane flying high over the city, surveying the damage done during the first raid and preparing the ground for the next one . . .

It came that evening, when around 200 bombers left their bases in Northern France and the Low Countries and headed for Northern Ireland; they included Heinkel 111s, Junkers 88s and Dorniers, the latter capable of carrying a bomb-load of 3,300 lbs.

The sirens sounded at 10.40 p.m. and, as before, the first planes dropped flares to light up the target area.

They were followed by more waves of planes carrying incendiaries, high-explosive bombs and land-mines. From then until 5 o'clock the following morning, bombs continued to fall inexorably all around the shipyard area. By 4 a.m., the entire north of the city appeared to be ablaze.

As soon as the Irish Government heard of the air raids, de Valera immediately issued instructions that all available fire-fighting units from Eire be sent across the border to help fight the fires: 'They are our own people, after all,' he said.

Later, speaking at Castlebar on 20 April, de Valera said:

> I know you will wish me to express on your behalf, on behalf of the Government, our sympathy with the people who are suffering . . . In the past, and probably in the present, too, a number of them did not see eye to eye with us politically, but they are our people – we are one and the same people – and their sorrows in the present instance are also our sorrows; and I want to say to them that any help we can give to them in the present time we will give to them whole-heartedly, believing that were the circumstances reversed they would also give us their help whole-heartedly . . .'

In all, thirteen fire brigade units from Dublin, Dun Laoghaire, Dundalk and Drogheda travelled up to the North, and worked for two days and nights until they were sent back by the Northern Ireland Government for fear that another raid – which seemed imminent – would make the Irish Government's problem even more difficult, since the sending of fire-brigades to assist a belligerent country could be regarded as a breach of the neutrality regulations.

By that time, almost 900 people had been killed and another 1,500 injured, 400 of them seriously. The extent of the raid had taken Belfast completely by surprise. The hospitals were able to treat the casualties only under the most trying conditions, plainly over-stressed by the numbers involved, and the city morgue was completely unable to cope with the constant flow of bodies. In the Falls Road baths, bodies were first laid out around the swimming pool, but when coffins ran out they were eventually accommodated in the swimming pool itself; during the week-end following the bombing, there was a public funeral for 150 of the dead, 123 of them still unidentified and all buried in a mass grave.

At 11.45 p.m. on the night of 4 May, the Belfast air-raid sirens sounded again. This time the planes didn't bother to drop flares, but the first bombs started to fall a few minutes after 1 o'clock in the morning, and they were mostly incendiaries. Estimates made after the raid reckoned that the bombers dropped over 200 metric tonnes of high explosive and about 96,000 incendiary bombs.

Major damage was inflicted on the harbour area, the shipyards and the aircraft factories. No other ship-yard in the United Kingdom had been so devastated

'amon de Valera had wanted his country to be neutral and neutral it stayed, in one of
ae greatest diplomatic feats of the Second World War.'
im Pat Coogan in *De Valera: Long Fellow, Long Shadow*

On September 4 1939 – the second day of The Emergency – the *SS Athenia* was sunk b
a German submarine in the Atlantic and 450 survivors were landed at Galway, bringin
a glimpse of the harsh realities of war to neutral Ireland.

A pre-war picture of Dublin tram-cars at their city terminal, Nelson's Pillar, now gon
The trams were due to have been phased out around 1941, but were retained in servi
until 1944, because of the shortage of petroleum fuels.

Hulton-Deutsch

Many of Ireland's lorries and motor cars were fitted with producer-gas units and adapted to run on a gas made from coal, or coal and wood, or even wood and turf.

Hulton-Deutsch

Others were adapted to run on town gas, supplied by many garages, which had installed special pumps for the purpose, and stored in a rubberised-fabric 'tank' on the roof.

Many city-dwellers bought or rented plots of bogland in the surrounding countryside and spent their weekends digging and stacking turf for their own use when coal supplies dried up.

Turf to keep Dublin's home fires burning during The Emergency was stacked on both sides of the Long Straight in Phoenix Park, now rechristened the New Bog Road.

ıroughout the war years, German planes regularly crashed or crash-landed on Irish rritory. All surviving airmen were interned in the Curragh Camp in Co. Kildare 'for e duration'.

ımb damage in the centre of Belfast city. In April and May 1941, over a thousand ɔple were killed in two heavy air raids which also severely damaged the shipyards d aircraft factories.

On May 31 1941, German bombers, deflected from Belfast by British radar, dropped
couple of land mines on the North Strand area of Dublin, killing 28 and leaving 2,5
people homeless.

The battle of Agincourt, from Laurence Olivier's film of Shakespeare's Henry V, shot
the estates of Lord Powerscourt in Enniskerry, Co. Wicklow, in the summer of 1943.

C. A. Duncan

...avid Gray,
...e American Ambassador to Eire.

Sir John Maffey,
the British Representative.

Tony Gray

...chting, on an extravagant, pre-war style, flourished in neutral Ireland during The
...nergency and there were regattas in Dublin Bay most weekends during the sailing
...ason.

When private motoring came to an end in 1941, pony traps, cabs, side-cars and eve
stage coaches began to appear on the Irish road. Here a party of young Dubliners a
seen jaunting up O'Connell Street on a side-car.

in the course of one night. It was six months before the yard returned to full production, and if anybody wonders why Belfast was not raided again, the simple explanation is that every important factory or industrial site in the area had been either wiped out or very seriously incapacitated.

Casualties were low compared with the previous raid, however. Only 150 people had been killed and 157 seriously injured, probably partly as the result of the evacuation – in part to Eire – of more than 100,000 people and partly to a great improvement in anti-aircraft defences which forced the bombers to fly at twice the altitude used during the two previous raids.

At 4.35 a.m. the all-clear was sounded and people ventured out into the streets to assess the damage. Once again, the arrival of fire-brigade units from across the border in Eire – though uninvited – had helped to hold the flames back.

The following night, 5–6 May, the air-raid warnings again sounded. Three or four bombers, possibly strays from a major raid on the Clyde shipbuilding area, dropped a few bombs on the city, killing about a dozen people.

In all, 191 people had been killed in the two May raids. The seriously injured totalled 186, with a further 615 slightly wounded. As with the April raid, there was a public mass funeral and a communal grave.

And – possibly also because by June Hitler had decided to abandon his attempt to invade Britain and turn his attention instead upon the Russians – there were no further air raids on Belfast. However, reference should be made to the dropping of a land-mine on the North Strand area of Dublin – not very far from the docks – on the night of 31 May 1941, and of a number of bombs in the Dublin area by German bombers who (as we now know) were given to believe that they were yet again over Belfast, finishing off the job, as a result of British interference with the wireless rays or radar beams which the pilots used to navigate at night. According to Dermot Keogh's *Twentieth Century Ireland* (Dublin: Gill & Macmillan, 1994), 'this was confirmed after the war by the British Air Ministry, and reports were carried in the Dublin newspapers on 23 February 1946.'

However, although the British may have been morally responsible for the death and destruction caused in the raid, because they had deliberately deflected the radio beams to direct the aircraft towards Dublin rather than Belfast, the bombs that did the damage were undoubtedly German, and the Germans accepted the responsibility and paid the Irish Government £327,000 compensation in 1958.

I was in the Editorial Department of the *Irish Times* when the first bombs fell in the Dublin area on the night of 31 May to 1 June, around 2 o'clock in the morning. With Smyllie and Newman, I hurried down the main stairs to the front office, and out into Westmoreland Street. As none of the previous German bombs which had dropped on Ireland had done very much damage, we didn't take this raid very seriously. In fact, on his way out into Westmoreland Street, Smyllie seized a tin-hat which was kept as part of the air-raid precaution arrangements in the *Irish Times* front office, and jammed it on his head, grabbing a broom which stood beside it and using this like a rifle in the slope-arms position. He had inevitably, at this time of the morning, some drink taken, as they say.

We had only been outside for a few moments when there was a huge flash in the sky followed by an enormous 'crump' sound, the kind of explosion you feel as pressure against your chest rather than actually hear. I have only had exactly the same experience once since then, and that was just before Christmas 1983, when my wife and I were in Harrods when an IRA bomb exploded in the street below, killing five people and wounding a hundred. Smyllie, who knew what bombs sounded like, turned white, took off the helmet and said, 'Gentlemen. They are not joking. That was a very big one. Gray, as the only young and able-bodied member of the Editorial Department, kindly go and offer your services at once as a volunteer reporter to the news department of this newspaper.'

He led the way back into the office and returned the helmet and the broom to the ARP station. I collected my coat, because it was quite chilly, and reported to the news room. The night town man – Sammy Bestic – had already left the office and was heading in the direction of the explosion, and one of the junior subs was in temporary charge of the Reporters' Room until the half-dozen reporters who had been called in arrived. I told him that I had been ordered by the Editor to report for duty, and he suggested that it might not be a bad idea if I cycled up to the Zoological Gardens as they'd heard from the police that a bomb had fallen on the Zoo and that some of the animals had escaped.

When I cycled up to the normal Zoo entrance it was closed, as I should have expected it would be at 2.45 a.m., but I knew the way around the side, through what might be described as the service entry. There were a lot of lights on in the area, and I learned from one of the attendants that a North American bison (caged just inside the main door behind iron bars stout enough to restrain an elephant) had taken fright at the sound of the bombs, put his head down and bashed his way out of his enclosure into freedom within the Zoological Gardens enclosure, from which he could have escaped out into Phoenix Park, but he didn't bother.

Apparently a bomb had fallen in the area of the Dog Pond pumping station, just outside the Zoo perimeter, and the blast had not only shattered all the windows in the house of Cedric Flood, the Zoo Super-intendent, but also (I learned later) all the windows in Arus an Uachtarain, the residence of President Douglas Hyde.

Inside the Zoo, the one remaining elephant had been knocked over by the blast – or had decided that it was safer to lie down perhaps – and refused even to attempt to get to his feet again until the arrival of his friend, Cedric Flood, wearing a dressing-gown over his pyjamas. The monkeys were creating a terrible fuss and upsetting all the other animals.

However, as it was clear that nobody had been killed or injured in the Phoenix Park area, I phoned the office, told them what had happened at the Zoo and then cycled into town again, heading for what appeared to be a huge fire which was lighting up the entire sky. It was now about 3.30 a.m.

As I drew close to the bombed area – the North Strand district of Dublin – I left my bicycle against some railings and walked the rest of the way. There was an LSF/ARP cordon around the whole area, and although it was nearly two hours since the bomb (which turned out to be a land-mine) had fallen, bodies were still being recovered from the dozen or so shattered buildings.

In the darkness and confusion, it was impossible to gain any impression of what had happened and, understandably, the LDF and ARP men on duty – much less the police and soldiers who were also there – had no time to talk to the press, not that they knew very much more about it anyway. From time to time, there were crashes from the bombed houses as staircases and partition walls collapsed in showers of fiery sparks, and while I stood just outside the cordon, two ambulance men came out carrying a stretcher.

I had seen dead bodies before, but not like this. As part of my general education as a newspaperman,

Smyllie had insisted that I should attend an inquest at the City Morgue. I was to have gone with the reporter covering it, but turned up late to find that he had gone in ahead of me. Once inside, I took the wrong door and found myself in the mortuary, surrounded by several pale bodies lying flat on their backs on marble slabs. I couldn't help noticing that their torsos had been slashed from navel to neck and then hastily sewn up again with what looked like garden twine.

But the body now on the stretcher appeared to be covered in what looked like a coating of fine ash, though it could have been dust – everything seemed to be covered in the dust of centuries – and when the stretcher-bearers passed under a street-light, there were rivulets of what looked like purple tar oozing from the ash. The body was obviously smashed beyond recognition; you couldn't even tell whether it was man, woman or child.

One of the collapsed houses had an open piano seemingly clinging to the wall of a third-floor room, except that there was no floor and no room . . . it just hung there as if suspended from a picture hook, with an open sheet of music still propped up in the music rest, an unforgettable sight.

Correctly assuming that I would not be able to discover anything of value on the spot, apart perhaps from some vague general impressions of the scene, I went back to the Reporters' Room at the office, where Matt Chambers, the deputy Chief Reporter, was sitting at his typewriter, surrounded by other reporters who were dictating to him what they had been able to discover about the events of the night. He was writing it all down on those half-quarto slips of waste newsprint which the subs and reporters used all the time; it was known as copy-paper. As it came out of his typewriter, Matt Chambers handed the material, page by page, to a rewrite sub, who sorted it all out into some sort of a coherent narrative; the presses were constantly stopped throughout the morning in order to incorporate the latest version of the story.

As I had suspected when I was at the scene, nobody there had any idea how many people had been killed or injured. The only certain way to get any firm figures was from the city hospitals and when the final edition came out at about 9 o'clock on Saturday morning, 1 June, it reported that over a hundred people had been taken to Jervis Street Hospital, and there were five dead in the Mater Hospital. At least seventeen houses had been destroyed by the land-mine which fell on the North Strand, another bomb had fallen in the North Circular Road, one or more in the Ballybough area, and another had demolished two houses, Nos. 43 and 44, at Summerhill Parade, almost exactly opposite the O'Connell Schools. And, of course, there was the bomb in the Phoenix Park.

By this time it was far too late to think about going home to bed, so Sammy Bestic and I went back to the North Strand to see what the scene looked like in daylight, and to collect some more material for a follow-up story for Monday's paper. By the time we arrived the last of the bodies appeared to have been removed, though there was still an LSF cordon around the area to keep the crowds back. The land-mine had fallen bang in the middle of the cobbled road, between the tramlines, and had left a crater at least eight feet deep. As well as some 20 to 25 houses which had been completely demolished, there was considerable damage to an undertaker's parlour – it was in fact the parlour featured in the funeral in James Joyce's *Ulysses* – to Fagan's pub at the corner of North William Street, to Corcoran's Dairies and a chemist's shop. The crater near the O'Connell Schools was at least 20 yards wide, but not very deep; it seemed that the bomb had exploded on impact.

By Monday we were able to piece together a fairly coherent account of the night's events; the final toll was 32 dead and over 80 injured, many seriously.

In these days of on-the-spot television reportage of wars, earthquakes and other disasters, we are all inured to the sight of the injured, the dead and dying, but in those times the newspapers never printed photographs of dead bodies, and I found the whole experience utterly shattering.

8

><<><

BACK TO BASICS

There doesn't seem to be any close connection between turf and transportation, but in Ireland during The Emergency there was.

Apart from some scattered woods and a few minute deposits of anthracite coal at Castlecomer, near Kilkenny, in the Arigna coalfields in Co. Leitrim and some disused coal-mines at Slieve Ardagh in Co. Tipperary – which the Government hastily took over in February 1941, though to no great effect – the only indigenous fuel in Ireland when the Second World War broke out was turf, or, as it is known in England, peat.

Turf is a brown, spongy substance, composed of plant fibres compressed by the centuries into something half-way between a sod of earth and a chunk of tree bark. It looks as inflammable as a sod of earth, which it very nearly is. Properly treated, it will smoulder away gently, producing a pleasant smell, a lot of smoke and a little, very gentle heat.

Here is Patrick Campbell's account of one attempt to use the stuff as a domestic fuel, taken from the column he wrote in the *Irish Times* just after the war, when we were still forced to use the wretched stuff as fuel because there was nothing else available to keep the home fires burning:

'What I love about your Dublin,' said the foreign visitor, 'is the heavenly smell of peat.'

'Pete who?' I said, twisting another newspaper into strips and poking it into the fire, lying flat on my face, with my eyes running.

'Peat,' said the visitor. 'The stuff you're lighting.'

I blew madly into the fire, until the room began to swirl around. 'It's not called peat,' I said. 'It's called turf.'

The foreigner thought for a moment, and then he said: 'But how do you light it?'

I gave one final blast, and threw the bellows into the fire. 'You take four bundles of sticks,' I said, 'and dry them in a gas oven until crisp. While the sticks are drying, you dry a quarter of a ton of turf, piece by piece, on an electric stove. Set the fire and touch a match to it, and then start rushing up and down the back stairs carrying up more and more turf and flinging it into the fire until it's time to go to bed.'

The foreign visitor looked uncomfortable, and

then he said: 'I suppose, actually, you're probably joking.'

But he wasn't joking. A bog in its natural state is 95
per cent water. How about that for a potential fuel,
and the only indigenous one in what is often one
of the chilliest countries in the European Union? It
didn't matter greatly in peacetime, when the British
were only too anxious to export coal to Ireland,
but it became of paramount importance during The
Emergency when they needed all the decent coal they
could mine for the war effort.

As early as 1933, the Irish Government had been
taking a long, cool look at this unpromising material
to see whether there wasn't a more intelligent and
economical way of exploiting it other than the traditional method of digging it up, propping it up in
stooks to dry out a bit in what little sunshine they
get in Ireland, even in a good year, and then putting
it on the fire in the forlorn hope that it may burn.

They set up a Turf Development Board, which
began its activities by establishing a cooperative mar-
keting board to ensure a better distribution of all the
turf that was currently being privately cut. 'This was
during the period of the Economic War,' a Turf Board
man remembers, 'when the slogan was, "Burn everything British except her coal", and the shortcomings
of turf as a domestic fuel were far less important than
the fact that it didn't come from England.'

However, as soon as they started distributing the
stuff, the Turf Development people saw that the old,

hand-won turf was utterly unsuited to commercial exploitation. It varied enormously in quality, according to which area it came from and the length of time and manner in which it had been laid out to dry. It was very bulky for its weight, and if you bought hand-won turf by the sack, as most people did in those days, you had no way of knowing what weight you were getting or whether the weight, if the sack happened to be heavy, was solid, hard, fiercely-burning turf of top quality, or merely an extra ration of water.

Prior to the war, the Government had started to look around at other countries plagued with large quantities of peat and turf instead of soil, and had sent survey teams to Germany and Russia to study the various methods of mechanisation they had been trying out. Basically, what they were seeking was some means of standardising the quality and increasing the calorific value of turf, and some way of exploiting it on a national, industrial scale. By the time war broke out they were already considering various techniques for scraping the surface of the bog mechanically, then compressing and baking the turf dust into briquettes of a consistent weight, density and calorific content. These briquettes proved such a success that they continued to sell very well long after The Emergency ended; indeed they still sell well today, even in England, where they are bought by Irish emigrants lucky enough still to have open fires, partly because they are far cleaner than coal or coke and partly because the aroma reminds the emigrants of the 'ould sod'. Almost by accident, it was also discovered that turf dust makes an excellent potting compound, so you can find sacks of Irish peat moss at any garden centre in England and indeed all over the world today; it became a very profitable and highly exportable sideline.

The Irish Government's Turf Development Board also considered ways of burning the turf dust scraped off the surface of the bogs in a furnace to produce electricity; I mentioned earlier that the 1940 Electricity Bill included a sum of £800,000 for the construction of an experimental turf-burning power station to be built on the Clonsast bog, near Portarlington. Before the end of The Emergency this power station was up and running and contributing power to the national grid.

The development of turf, both as a domestic fuel and as a source of power, became of vital importance when war broke out and Britain began to restrict supplies of coal to Eire to small and infrequent consignments of such a low grade that it was almost incombustible. You couldn't blame Britain; she needed all the decent coal her miners could dig up for the manufacture of weapons and armaments. But, equally, there is no doubt that Britain was gently rebuking Ireland for her impertinent rejection of Dominion status by restricting essential supplies in a way that also emphasised and underlined Ireland's dependence on the UK.

The appointment of Sean Lemass as Minister for Supplies was probably the brightest thing de Valera did at the outbreak of hostilities; Lemass was persuasive enough to coax the British into supplying enough essential commodities such as tea, which would have been unobtainable without her help. Eire had made her own arrangements to buy tea in India, Ceylon and elsewhere, and normally bought far better tea than Britain did, but as she had no ships in which to transport it – or anything else, for that matter – to Ireland, it had always arrived via England in British vessels. Lemass was able to persuade the British to supply Ireland with small consignments of many essential commodities, including tea; he was also resourceful enough to set up a state-controlled Irish Shipping Company.

In the great days of the sailing schooners, Ireland's ports were always crowded with ships, many of them owned and operated by Irish firms. But when steam began to take over from sail, the cost of building ships went up sharply – and this at a time when capital was desperately short in Ireland and when, in any event, Ireland was being run from Westminster, and British policy was to direct all cargoes as far as possible into British vessels. So the sailing ships were not replaced, and Irish importing and exporting firms chartered space on British ships. This worked well enough in peacetime, and when the new state was formed in 1922 the provision of shipping did not appear to be a priority. Nor indeed was it during the first eighteen months of the war; there was still plenty of space available on British ships.

It was only when the submarine war began to

take a heavy toll of British shipping in 1941, and Britain needed all the shipping-space she had at her disposal to feed her own people, that the tonnage allocated to neutral Ireland quite understandably began to dwindle away and finally almost disappeared altogether. Under US neutrality legislation, American vessels were not allowed to enter Irish ports; and the supply of neutral ships ran out as one by one the neutral countries were overrun and became involved in the war.

Suddenly it became a question, quite simply, of keeping up the supply of grain to Ireland. As a result of the Fianna Fail policy of switching over from ranching to tillage, which was intensified as soon as the war broke out, the country was growing a great deal more grain than it had been ten years earlier, but still not enough to feed the population. Also, the climate is too uncertain to depend entirely on home-produced grain for the nation's bread supplies. So, as well as introducing a number of measures to cut down on bread consumption – for example, one Order made it illegal for hotels and restaurants to serve bread with more than one course at any meal – the Irish Government decided that it must get hold of some ships.

Irish Shipping Ltd was formed in March 1941, financed by the Government, and Sean Lemass and his very energetic and capable secretary, John Leydon, began to scour the world for anything capable of floating which could be bought, bartered or commandeered.

The first ship to be purchased abroad was a Greek vessel, the *Vassilos Destounis*, which had been discovered lying almost derelict in the Spanish port of Avila. She had been salvaged by Spanish fishermen after her crew had abandoned her during a German air attack at the time of the Spanish Civil War. Everything portable, including the radio, had been removed, she was leaking badly; the engines broke down on the first leg of the journey; and the mainmast collapsed when her Irish crew attempted to load her with grain. But in spite of all vicissitudes, the ship eventually reached harbour in the port of Dublin with a cargo of grain, and was renamed the *Irish Poplar*. However, she was not the first of the Irish Shipping Ltd vessels to do so: on 4 September 1941, one of two ships bought in America (and renamed the *Irish Elm*) arrived with a cargo of 7,000 tons of grain. As early as May an Irish crew had travelled to New Jersey on board a neutral ship to take over the *Leda of Panama* and supervise the refit, and on 7 December the *Irish Pine*, another vessel bought in America, arrived in Dublin port with a further cargo of grain from the States.

All the vessels of Irish Shipping Ltd carried the names of indigenous Irish trees, and they included one Latvian and three Estonian ships stranded in Irish ports at the outbreak of war and commandeered by the Government for the company. A Soviet claim to the ownership of these vessels was rejected by the Supreme Court on the grounds that the Government of Eire did not recognise the Government of the USSR as the sovereign government of Latvia and Estonia.

Other ships were bought and chartered in the United States and elsewhere, a derelict shipyard in Cork was reopened and refitted, and the Government spent huge sums refurbishing and repairing all manner of wrecks, at least one of which had paid a brief visit to the bottom of the sea.

Money to do this was borrowed from the banks, on a Government guarantee. In all, fifteen hulks were acquired and rendered seaworthy enough to undertake long sea voyages in search of grain and other vital supplies; not a very impressive merchant fleet, in all conscience, but sufficient for the purpose. The ships were so slow that they were a danger to convoys and had to travel on their own, brightly floodlit, with the Irish tricolour and the word EIRE prominently and proudly painted on the sides of their hulls.

When it came to coal, however, there was nothing Lemass could do, and early in 1941 the Government had to face a very serious situation. Believing it unthinkable that supplies of coal would ever run out – they never had before – the Irish fuel merchants had continued to supply all the orders that came in until, in January 1941, they suddenly noticed that almost all their reserves were gone and no further supplies were arriving. On 25 January, the Department of Supplies issued an Order limiting every household to half a ton of coal per month, at a time when domestic central heating was unheard of in Ireland; indeed, many of the smaller hotels and offices were at this period still heated only by open fires or electric radiators. At the same time, the public were urged to burn turf instead of coal wherever possible.

In a broadcast to the nation at the end of January, de Valera pointed out that Ireland was an island, effectively cut off from the rest of the world, and added: 'We can be sure of nothing that we do not produce ourselves'; in February the Government set up an Emergency Research Bureau to examine ways of using native substitute materials in as many applications as possible.

In March, the coal ration was cut to a quarter of a ton per household per month, and Frank Aiken, Minister for the Coordination of Defensive Measures, was dispatched to America (via Lisbon and the Azores) in the hope that he could secure some arms and ammunition for Ireland's expanding defence forces; he was also to inquire into the possibility of acquiring some coal, and various other scarce commodities. He was safely back in Ireland when on 20 May America's answer came through; the US Government was prepared to supply some food and two ships – one of which became the SS *Irish Pine*, mentioned above – through the Irish Red Cross Society, but no munitions. There was also a vague promise of some coal at a later period.

In July Hugo Flinn, formerly Parliamentary Secretary to the Department of Finance, who had been appointed Turf Controller, told the Dail that 30,000 workers were currently engaged in cutting 100,000 tons of turf per week; they had cut 550,000 tons since they started in May, and the Government had set up camps to provide temporary living quarters for them. There were in addition about 15,000 men cutting turf under various parish council and county council schemes, as well as voluntary bodies from the defence forces, and their output to date had been 200,000 tons.

By this time there was no coal whatever for sale in Dublin; and although plenty of turf had been cut, it still had to be dried and transported up to Dublin. Meanwhile, only very small supplies were available in the city: customers were limited to one-fifth of a ton, at a price of 11s (55p). If you wanted a decent fire, one-fifth of a ton would hardly last much longer than a week.

The GSR (Great Southern Railway) announced 'an extensive curtailment of services' including a considerable reduction in Sunday seaside trains. The DUTC (Dublin United Tramways Company) followed with an announcement that it would be compelled to make substantial reductions in its bus services because of the fuel shortage; proposals for retaining the staff on a rotational basis were under consideration. The Gas Company weighed in with the news that the calorific value of town gas was being drastically reduced; meals would take a lot longer to cook, and gas-fires would emit considerably less heat. It was probable that some form of gas rationing would follow, though at this stage nobody had any idea how this could be achieved.

By August, more cuts in the transport services were being announced. The GSR reported that it had only two weeks' supply of coal left, and was cutting services to one train per day on all the principal lines. The DUTC decided that there would be no buses after 11 p.m., and all cinemas and theatres were ordered to close by 10.30 p.m. The trams had been scheduled to be taken out of service before the war, but were retained because of the petroleum shortage.

Experiments were carried out into the possibilities of running trains on turf, or a mixture of turf and coal. Some GSR buses were converted to run on town gas, others on producer gas manufactured (in a trailer towed behind them) from Irish anthracite coal from the Castlecomer colliery. The GNR diesel buses were also converted to run on producer gas, manufactured from Northern Ireland (British) coal in a trailer. Many private motorists fitted their cars with similar producer units at a cost of between £50 and £80; they, too, ran on gas produced from coal when they could get it, or from a mixture of turf and wood, in a unit towed behind the car on a trailer. Other motorists had large oblong gas tanks of rubberised fabric fitted to the roofs of their cars, which had been adapted – with the aid of a second carburettor – to enable them to switch between petrol and town gas at a similar cost; town gas was available from many garages, which had invested in gas-metering equipment and nozzles for filling the tanks.

In August, the farmers sent a deputation to the Government to warn them that they would require a special ration of coal for the season's threshing operations; the harvest promised to be a bumper one.

It was: in July, Dr Ryan, Minister for Agriculture, told the Dail that the wheat crop would be the biggest since 1847, and the general harvest the biggest ever. The farmers were allowed some coal for beginning operations; but once they got the threshing machines started, they would have to keep them going on turf and wood.

In August, too, the GSR reported that the inferior coal with which they were being supplied was causing delays: the fireboxes of the locomotives kept going out. On 15 August, a GSR advertisement in the national newspapers apologised to the public for the disorganisation of their services, owing to the poor quality of the coal with which they were now being supplied. A few days later, a passenger train which left Cork at 2 p.m. and was due to arrive in Skibbereen at 4 p.m., did not arrive until 4 a.m. the following day, having taken 14 hours to cover 53 miles; the firebox had gone out several times, and on each occasion it had taken hours to get it started again.

In September the full significance of the domestic fuel situation was revealed in the Dail: in a normal winter, Dublin required 750,000 tons of top-quality coal; to produce an equivalent amount of heat and power would require at least 2,000,000 tons of wood and turf. The turf ration for non-turf areas was fixed at half a ton for the months of September and October. On 4 September it was announced that there was only one week's supply of domestic coal left in Dublin, and little hope of getting any more.

The farmers held a mass meeting to demand whatever coal there was for the priority work of threshing the harvest, and got an extra 25 cwt per week for the period when threshing was in progress.

The GSR now reported on the experiments they had been carrying out, using turf instead of coal in their trains; a locomotive that required only three tons of coal to travel from Dublin to Cork had to use over nine tons of turf – plus 1½ tons of coal, which was absolutely essential to make the turf burn; in addition, it needed a second fireman to keep the firebox stoked up, and a couple of extra tenders to carry the turf. 'Sure you might as well be trying to burn sand' was the comment of one GSR engine driver, speaking of the mixture of turf and coal which had been causing delays on all rail services.

From September, the use of town gas for motor-cars was suddenly prohibited, much to the annoyance of motorists who had spent a lot of money on having their cars converted and gas bags fitted, and to garage proprietors who had converted their garages for the supply of metered town gas. Cars with gas producers were still permitted, but by this time – according to an estimate in the *Irish Independent* – at least two out of every five cars in Ireland were up on blocks in their garages, and would remain out of commission for the duration. This was probably just as well, because in February the Government had ordered that all road signs should be removed, in order to confuse German spies and (if they ever did decide to invade the country) the German armed forces. The amount of confusion that this order caused among the natives was to some extent ameliorated by the sharp reduction in the number of cars still on the roads.

Goffs, the bloodstock auctioneers, had been scouring the country for traps, side-cars and other horse-drawn vehicles and had managed to assemble a sufficient collection to hold an auction at their sales paddock in Ballsbridge in September. However, by now most people had settled for the bicycle as the most practical answer to their personal transportation problems, and a new sight appeared in Dublin and in some of the other Irish towns: bicycle parking centres, complete with attendants. This was necessary because by now no new bicycles were available, second-hand bicycles were prohibitively expensive and tyres and spare parts impossible to find, with the result that bicycle theft became the commonest crime.

Nevertheless, life went on more or less as normally, and the dancing craze continued unabated. You could dance in evening dress to the music of Billy Dingle or Jimmy Masson and his Orchestra in the Gresham Hotel every Saturday night from 8 p.m. until midnight, for 5s for the dance only and 9s 6d if you wished to have supper. The singer was Frankie Blowers, a Frank Sinatra imitator. Since a list of those attending all dances – the Gresham Saturday-night dances as well as staff and old school and charity dances and hunt balls – was required reading in Dublin, free tickets were available in all the newspaper offices for reporters prepared to collect a list of names from among those present. So as soon as I had managed to arrange a transfer from the Editorial Department of the *Irish Times* to the Reporters' Room, where the hours were far more flexible, I went dancing on those free tickets almost every night, always cycling with my tails tucked up under my seat on the saddle, and with my partner of the night either sitting on the crossbar or cycling alongside with her evening dress somehow tucked out of the way of the pedals.

The dances we danced were basically the same sort of routines that were then fashionable in London night-clubs like the Trocadero and Oddenino's: the quick-step, the slow foxtrot, the waltz and the occasional rhumba and tango, as well as the odd Irish set dance like 'The Waves of Tory' or 'The Walls of Limerick'. There were frequent Paul Joneses, which gave us all an opportunity to change partners for a few moments and dance with a total stranger, at a period when ballroom dancing offered far more opportunities for extremely close sexual contact than today's disco dancing. Smyllie always referred to these dancing excursions as 'belly-rubbing expedi-tions' and believed, rightly in my opinion, that the reason for ballroom dancing's great popularity in Ireland was that it allowed this measure of legitimate physical contact at a time when 'courting in the hedgerows' was frowned upon by the bishops; also, most Irish girls (and boys) continued to live with their parents in relatively small, overcrowded houses (overlooked by their numerous young brothers and sisters) until they left home for good to attend their own weddings, a situation which allowed very few opportunities for intimacy of even the most cursory kind indoors.

In September 1943, G.P. McCarthy, the Co. Clare Medical Officer of Health, gave it as his considered opinion that the prevalent craze for 'ballroom' dancing was probably helping to spread the TB infection.

If you didn't feel like getting into evening dress on Saturday night, there were informal dances, known as 'hops', in the pavilions of most tennis, rugby and hockey clubs in the suburbs. Here, the same facilities for what Smyllie called 'belly-rubbing' were provided for a nominal 2s 6d (12½p), and with no need to get into anything more formal than a sports coat and flannels, or a summer dress. Since stockings had disappeared, most Irish girls painted their legs with various cosmetic preparations to simulate stockings – and very sexy they looked, too.

And if it should be considered that I was in any way unusual or depraved in my enthusiasm for this particular form of diversion, let me quote a highly-respected former Taoiseach of Ireland, Garret FitzGerald, who, in his autobiography *All in a Life* (Dublin: Gill & Macmillan, 1991), wrote:

An element of student life in that period was the formal dance, most commonly in the Gresham Hotel and organised by the past pupils of a secondary school or by a charity, which included dinner during the evening. White tie and tails were appropriate for these occasions, with black tie for the dinnerless five-shilling Saturday-night dances . . .

A feature of these dances was that many of us travelled to and from them by bicycle, often with a girl on the crossbar, her ball-gown packed away in a carrier-basket; it was necessary for the girls to change at the dance if they were to have a safe bicycle journey home in a shorter skirt [that wasn't my experience; the girls I took to dances preferred to take their chances in their evening dresses, both ways]. Other forms of transport might be used. Joan (Mrs Garret FitzGerald) recalls an evening when, emerging from the Gresham, she saw three young men about to take off by horse-cab; her next morning's nine o'clock lecturer, the future Senator Alexis FitzGerald [a friend of ours], and the future Chief Justice Tom O'Higgins [my LDF commanding officer at the period] and Tom Crotty, a future county registrar, on top of the vehicle.'

In view of the fuel situation – in a city like Dublin where a lot of the cooking was still done on old-fashioned ranges which burned only coal or coke, and the rest was done by gas – the Government discussed the provision of community kitchens to provide hot meals at a nominal price for people unable to prepare food in their homes. These measures were ostensibly designed to offset privations caused by lack of fuel and transportation problems – available transport could only cope with 500 tons of fuel (turf and wood) a day, roughly one-fifth of Dublin's requirements – but they also reflected the poverty which still existed in Ireland, particularly in Dublin city and some of the larger towns.

Communal kitchens already established in Rathmines and Ringsend by well-meaning, far-sighted citizens were public, self-supporting, and not connected with any religious or philanthropic bodies. And a number of Dublin hoteliers and restaurateurs got together to form a Guild of Goodwill which opened a restaurant in Pearse Street, which from September started to provide a two-course lunch (known in Dublin as dinner) which on the opening day consisted of soup, roast beef and two veg and cost 9d. In September, too, the St John Ambulance Brigade set up a community kitchen – in effect a mobile canteen – at 46 Merrion Square, which was capable of catering for 1,500 people a day at nominal charges. The Sisters of Charity of St Vincent de Paul managed to provide penny dinners in Henrietta Lane, Dublin: 1d for a meat stew, a slice of bread and a mug of milk, while the Goodwill Restaurants also started to provide a take-away service: a pint of soup cost 4d.

In October Hugo Flinn, the Turf Controller, gave the Dail a report on the fuel situation: they now had between 500,000 and 600,000 tons of turf for the non-turf areas – more than they were able to transport or store. But at last a storage place was found: what used to be called the Long Straight in Phoenix Park, from the Grand Prix racing days. Turf first appeared in Phoenix Park in huge stacks on each side of this long, straight road on 6 November 1941; and further supplies continued to arrive right through the winter, transported from the turf-producing areas partly by canal, partly by train and partly by army lorries; for the Department of Defence had provided 100 lorries to drive to Galway to collect turf supplies for Dublin and deposit them in Phoenix Park. The Long Straight now acquired a different name; it became 'the new bog road'.

In October it was discovered what form gas rationing would take. It began in Cork city: supplies of gas were restricted to the periods between 7.30 a.m. – 2 p.m. and 6 p.m. – 9.30 p.m.: outside these hours, all domestic gas supplies were cut off. Rationing in Clonmel began a week later and followed the same pattern.

It was not until the same system of gas rationing was extended to Dublin the following year that the canny Dubliners discovered that a 'glimmer' of gas remained in the pipes for hours after the supply had been cut, and that this could be used to heat a can of soup, boil water for a pot of tea or a hot toddy . . . and a new profession – the glimmer man – was born.

The dreaded glimmer man was an official employed by the Gas Company to snoop around the suburbs, spying on the citizens using the glimmer of gas that remained in the pipes during unpermitted hours; penalties for infractions included fines and disconnection. Incidentally, the way the glimmer man operated was simplicity itself; he simply placed his hand over the gas rings to feel whether they were hot or cold.

9

❧❧❧❧

BLUE PENCIL NIGHTS

As if the desperate shortage of fuel and the almost total disappearance of public transport were not enough for one year, Ireland – or rather, Ireland's cattle – suffered during 1941 from one of the worst attacks of foot-and-mouth disease the country had ever experienced. It began with an outbreak in Co. Derry on 17 January; Britain immediately stopped all cattle imports from Ireland, and before long all hunting and coursing fixtures were banned, the St Patrick's Day Dog Show had been cancelled, and by 25 February the Government had even banned walking in the mountains because of the danger of spreading the disease.

By the end of February, the seriousness of the situation was acknowledged and all fairs throughout the country were prohibited as well as most race-meetings. The Dublin Cattle Markets didn't open again until 11 July, after the longest closure (five months) in history. By then it was reckoned that the outbreak had cost the country over £223,000 in lost exports, and over 27,000 animals had been destroyed. But by September, everything was back to normal and Britain was taking more Irish beef than ever, although it wasn't until 16 October that the Northern Ireland Government, always lagging behind Britain in any concessions to the Republicans, lifted its ban on live cattle from Eire.

Another serious problem threatened Ireland's peace of mind around the same period: the possibility that conscription might be extended to include Northern Ireland.

Early in 1939 there had been something of a crisis when the then British Prime Minister, Neville Chamberlain, told the Commons that the Government intended to introduce compulsory military service. Mr de Valera, due to sail to New York to open the Irish Pavilion at the World's Fair, postponed his visit 'because of certain grave events'. Everybody knew that he was talking about the possible effects of conscription on Northern Ireland.

Theoretically, there was no reason why conscription should not apply equally to Northern Ireland, since it was regarded – at any rate by the British and by the Ulster Unionists – as an integral part of the United Kingdom. At the same time, the Catholic Nationalists – who numbered about one-third of the population of the Six Counties – could hardly be expected to take kindly to the idea of being forced to fight for a regime which had placed an artificial border between them and their fellow-countrymen. And even if the Catholic Nationalists did not resist conscription by force of arms, there was always the danger that the IRA might act on their behalf. The six Catholic bishops whose dioceses lie within the Six-County area issued a statement saying that they were convinced that any attempt to impose conscription in Northern Ireland would be disastrous, and the British Government would lose more than they would gain if they imposed it. Lord Craigavon crossed over to London to urge the British Government to press on with conscription, though he must have known the trouble it would cause. In the Dail, de Valera spoke of the measure as 'an act of aggression'. Two days later, Chamberlain announced that conscription would not apply to Northern Ireland.

But the matter arose again, when the British were sorely pressed following the collapse of the Low Countries and the Fall of France. In May 1941, another attempt to extend conscription to Northern Ireland was once again warmly welcomed by the Northern Unionists and stoutly resisted by de Valera. On 26 May, de Valera protested against conscription in Northern Ireland on the grounds that the Six Counties were a part of Ireland and that it would be an outrage for them to be forced to fight for Britain. Churchill decided that it would probably be more trouble than it was worth to attempt to extend conscription to Northern Ireland, and the matter was dropped for the remainder of the war, though by October thousands of US technicians and workmen were busy building a Lease-Lend Base in Northern Ireland under the protection of a body of US Marines; a US official said that a large area of Northern Ireland was now under American control, and that a protecting force was necessary.

This was a period during which there was a great deal of criticism both from the newspapers themselves – with the exception, naturally, of the *Irish Press*, largely owned by the de Valera family and the official organ of de Valera's Fianna Fail party – and from the Opposition in the Dail and Senate, about the way in which the Government had been operating the new press censorship. Following a major debate about the Government's use of the press censorship mechanism for political means in the Dail and Senate in 1940, the subject was again raised in 1941.

Press censorship was introduced at the outbreak of war, primarily as a means of ensuring that nothing would appear in the Irish newspapers which might imperil or endanger Ireland's neutrality, but the man in charge was Frank Aiken, Minister for the Coordination of Defensive Measures, who may have been a stout freedom fighter but was not one of the brightest or most sensitive of men and soon started to use the censor's blue pencil to give expression to a number of his own personal preferences. For example, he objected to the newspapers using the title of the organisation known as the Royal National Lifeboat

Institution; he argued that if it was 'Royal' it could not also be 'National' and refused to accept that if this was the official name of the Institution concerned, that was the end of the matter.

Censorship was organised into three divisions, postal, telegraphic and press, all controlled by a chief censor who was a civil servant, and all answerable to Frank Aiken whose judgement, as F.H. Boland commented, 'was not his long suit'. The Chairman of the Board of Works, Joseph Connolly, served as Controller of Censorship until September 1941, when he was replaced by one of his assistant controllers, Thomas Coyne, from the Department of Justice. A former journalist, Michael Knightly, was Chief Press Censor.

It seemed to me – working with Smyllie and Newman in the Editorial Department of the newspaper in the period between the autumn of 1940 and the summer of 1942 – that the activities of the Irish Press Censor were sharply stepped up in the wake of the fall of France, and in a way, with hindsight, that seems quite understandable. If Britain were to collapse as suddenly as the Low Countries and France had done, the Irish Government – and in particular, Frank Aiken and those responsible for the coordination of defensive measures – must have realised that before long they might find themselves having to answer questions posed not by mild officials from the British Dominions Office, but by a stern, implacable resident German *Gauleiter*; and from those dark days onwards, the whole approach to press censorship appeared to change.

From the moment Paris fell, a series of epic battles took place almost nightly (no pun intended) between Messrs Knightly and Coyne on the one hand, and Messrs Smyllie and Newman on the other. For a start, all references to Irishmen serving with the British forces were now banned. Probably the best-known war story about Smyllie is when Johnny Robinson, one of my predecessors in that cubby-hole behind Smyllie's office, went down with the *Prince of Wales* somewhere off Singapore. The only way that Smyllie could get the news of his rescue across to his readers was in these terms:

> The many friends of Mr John A. Robinson, who was involved in a recent boating accident, will be pleased to hear that he is alive and well. Mr Robinson, who is a native of Caledon, Co. Tyrone, was a member of the *Mid-Ulster Mail* for some years. He joined the *Irish Times* in 1934 and immediately left his mark on newspaper work . . . He is a particularly good swimmer, and it is possible that he owes his life to this accomplishment.

This paragraph appeared in the news pages on 17 December 1941, with a photograph of Johnny, and the headline 'ACCIDENT IN THE PACIFIC'.

As mentioned in the Introduction, Smyllie referred to other casualties as being for example 'in hospital suffering from lead poisoning incurred in the Libyan desert'. 'Lead poisoning' was his euphemism for a bullet wound, or shrapnel, and I cannot believe that men as intelligent as Coyne and Knightly were fooled by it for a moment; I think they probably enjoyed Smyllie's ingenuity, convinced that it would probably go unnoticed by their boss, Frank Aiken.

One incident which prompts me to this conclusion is the way in which they allowed Smyllie to break one of their principal rules relating to Irishmen serving with the British forces, particularly in key positions. Smyllie wanted to draw the attention of his readers to the fact that so many of the top Allied commanders in 1941 originally came from Ireland, North and South, and he did so by publishing the following paragraph in *An Irishman's Diary*:

In his broadcast on Sunday night, Mr Winston Churchill, the British Prime Minister (N.B. Britain is an island to the east of Eire), mentioned by name nine military and naval commanders who had gained fame recently in North Africa and in the Mediterranean. I append the names of the gallant nine:

General Wavell	English
General Mackie	Australian
General Wilson	Japanese (North Island)
General O'Connor	Japanese
General O'Moore Creagh	Japanese
General Dill	Japanese (North Island)
General Brooke	Japanese (North Island)
General Cunningham	Japanese
General Somerville	Japanese

As that venerable member of the samurai, San Tiok Eli [Sean T. O'Kelly, then Tanaiste, or Deputy Premier] might or might not have put it: *'Quae regio in terra non plena laboris?'*

In his biography of de Valera, Tim Pat Coogan quotes a description of how the censorship worked, written by Smyllie for *Foreign Affairs* (Washington: 1946):

Mr Frank Aiken ... was well-known for his anti-British feelings ... in theory the censorship was entirely neutral; in practice it worked almost exclusively against the Allies ... No paper dared to print a word in favour of the Allied cause. Even when the Americans came in, and Mr de Valera no longer had the excuse that it was mainly a British war, this rigid veto was maintained. Whether the Irish Government was trying to humbug the people of Eire, or was merely humbugging itself, nobody will ever know; but one thing is quite certain, it was not humbugging the Germans ... They knew that, with the insignificant exception of a small number of irreconcilables, the people of Southern Ireland were wholeheartedly on the side of the Allies ...

It is certainly true that on many occasions the paper was held up while the Art Editor was trying to find pictures to substitute for those killed by the

Press Censor. Alan Montgomery remembered that the paper was once forced to find a substitute for a harmless study of a pretty girl captioned: 'Spring comes to St Stephen's Green', which had been deleted on the grounds that the light summer dress worn by the girl might provide 'useful meteorological information to one or other of the combative forces'. This was so silly on the face of it that I can only think that the Censor's office was driven to despair by Smyllie's constant stratagems, some of which were pretty small-minded, and got their own back by making the *Irish Times* miss the newspaper train yet again.

Several members of the staff were quite certain that the paper was often kept late by the Censor's insistence on trivial changes of wording that had nothing whatever to do with any possible danger to Ireland's neutrality. For example, there was the refusal, to pass the word 'Kingstown' – even when it was used as the official name of a building, i.e. Kingstown Presbyterian Church, or Kingstown Grammar School, or as part of a quoted speech by a man who had in fact used the old term Kingstown – on the grounds that there was now no such place, and that it should be referred to as 'Dun Laoghaire'. Alan Montgomery also remembered the compulsory insertion of 'His Holiness' before the words 'the Pope' in a headline, which entailed a major rejig of the main news page.

The Opposition in the Dail and Senate always claimed that the debates were heavily censored, ostensibly for the sake of 'balance' (which was no part of the Press Censor's function anyway) but in fact, always to favour the Government (Fianna Fail) argument. Although nobody mentioned it during the debates in the Dail and Senate, because nobody in the Dail or Senate supported the IRA, the censorship system was also used to keep references to IRA activities and their repercussions – including deaths on hunger strike and executions – to a bare minimum.

To use the weapon of censorship for any reason other than to prevent the newspapers from printing stories which might endanger Ireland's neutrality was as illegal as it was dishonest, and to use it for political advantage was inexcusable, but the Irish were never very meticulous in their observance of the tenets of democracy. It would, of course, be highly unfair even to make such a suggestion if it were based solely on things said by members of the *Irish Times* staff who had suffered from the effects of the Censor's blue pencil. However, there was a big debate in the Senate in October 1940 about the abuse of power by the Press Censor, during the course of which some trivial but disgraceful affairs came to light. Senator Sir John Keane took up the matter and accused the Government of using press censorship to prevent any news reaching the public of the poisoning of the River Blackwater by effluents from a factory in Mallow, Co. Cork, owned by a Fianna Fail supporter. He also referred to a 'photograph of a well-known building in a city in this country – not identified, by order of the censor – the façade of which carried a historic emblem of the old days of the cruel Ascendancy', in front of which a monster recruiting rally for the LSF was taking place.

'When the photograph was submitted to the censor,' he added, 'it came back with instructions that the emblem of the Ascendancy should be removed.'

The emblem he was talking about was the Lion and Unicorn over a branch of the Bank of Ireland; the newspaper involved was the *Irish Times*, and the suggestion was made in the Senate that the editor of that newspaper had deliberately chosen a photograph in which this emblem was particularly prominent. This hardly seems likely, though it is just possible. Sir John Keane also objected to the fact that the Dail debates were subject to press censorship, and Senator Frank MacDermot added that it was dangerous that the Censor should have both complete secrecy and absolute power of control. He accused Frank Aiken, the minister responsible, of tampering with reports of Dail debates, and said that the government was censoring things not because they were endangering the safety of the state, but merely because the government did not like them.

In his reply, Aiken very foolishly alleged that one of the reasons why newspaper editors did not like press censorship was that before it came in, they had enjoyed the luxury of acting as press censors themselves. 'We are changing the function of the editor of the *Irish Times* and the other papers,' he announced, 'to myself and my staff. It is now we who have final say on what to cut out, not the editors.'

This remark naturally caused an uproar, and in January 1941 Senator MacDermot raised the matter in the Senate again, stating that the *Cork Examiner*, the *Irish Times* and the *Irish Independent* were all exceedingly dissatisfied with the way in which the censorship was being carried out. He added that the current storm about it had been set off by Aiken's stupid remark concerning the editors, and he wanted to put the record straight by pointing out that while one editor could certainly exercise a censorship function by cutting an item which he didn't like out of his own newspaper, he would have no control over the other newspapers, and in this way the public was protected. On the other hand, when the Censor decided that there was some item of news which he didn't personally like, he could cut it out of all of the newspapers and the public would never hear anything about it; and that, apart from the professional experience of the newspaper editors, was the chief difference between their function and that of Mr Frank Aiken.

There was a point, though it probably didn't arise until 1942, when matters between the Censor and the *Irish Times* reached a crucial stage. Normally everything was submitted in galley-proof form (that is to say, in the form of straight, single-column proofs of the material, which would later be fitted into the pages of the newspaper); but because Smyllie sometimes used very clever juxtapositions to point up anomalies between the comparatively comfortable and normal life in neutral Eire during The Emergency and the terrible effects of the Blitz in England, the Censor, for a period, insisted on seeing complete page proofs of all *Irish Times* pages. This obviously caused considerable delays and often resulted in the loss of thousands of copies in the country, because the newspaper trains would not wait indefinitely for the Censor to conclude his skirmishes with Smyllie. On this point, after a lengthy discussion with Coyne and Knightly, Smyllie gave in abruptly and (we all thought) uncharacteristically meekly, agreeing to stop playing games with them if they would in turn agree not to insist on seeing complete proofs of all pages as finally made up. After that, to everybody's surprise, Smyllie behaved extremely well and there was no more trouble.

Looking back, I think that Smyllie had begun to tire of the game. It had been great fun in the beginning, when censorship was a novelty and Knightly was on duty most evenings until quite late, so that he and Newman had an adversary worthy of their mettle with whom to argue. But as the war progressed, and as Knightly and his senior officers started to go home earlier and earlier and leave junior civil servants in charge of the shop, Smyllie didn't find it all that much fun exercising his intelligence against them, especially since the civil servants could always go by the book and were bound to win the game anyway. Furthermore, after Pearl Harbor victory for the Allies seemed only a matter of time, and Smyllie was prepared to wait.

He was, though none of us knew it, holding one

final trick up his sleeve, which he didn't release until the end of the war in Europe. But I won't spoil the story by referring to it in advance.

Books, records, plays and films were all subject to censorship. So far as films were concerned, the Film Censor was empowered to reject any film which, in his opinion, might prove prejudicial to the maintenance of law and order, or which might lead to a breach of the peace, or cause offence to the government and people of a friendly foreign nation. According to Dermot Keogh's *Twentieth-Century Ireland* (Dublin: Gill & Macmillan, 1994) Aiken took a keen personal interest in film censorship. Films considered unsuitable for showing included Charlie Chaplin's *The Great Dictator*, *Sergeant York*, and *Target for Tonight*. He goes on: 'Censorship decisions ranged from the farcical . . . to the highly serious, such as the suppression of reports of concentration camps and even the massacre of Irish missionaries in the Philippines.'

The disarray into which the IRA had fallen, largely as a result of the Government's strong-arm methods, was illustrated by a curious sequence of events which started with the appearance in the Dublin suburb of Rathmines of a half-crazed man with shackles around his ankles and a revolver in his hand. He staggered into the local police station on 8 September 1941, telling the police that he was the IRA Chief of Staff, Stephen Hayes, and that he had been held in captivity (by members of the IRA unknown to him) in various places for almost two months: beaten, interrogated, starved, prevented from sleeping and eventually tried by an IRA court martial, most of whose members were also complete strangers to him. After his trial he had been confined in a house in Castlewood Avenue, Rathmines, from which he had just that morning escaped, and where he had been forced to write a 'confession' dictated by a Sean McCaughey, who appeared to be an IRA officer of some kind. The police immediately sent a party round to Castlewood Avenue to investigate; in the course of the investigation one IRA man, James Rice of Belfast, was shot and died later in hospital, and two others escaped, one of them badly injured.

The full story did not come out until after the end of the war. Apparently, some of the younger members of the IRA, whom the wave of executions, shootings and internments had brought to the top of the movement, had come to the conclusion that the recent series of setbacks, arrests and internments had not been the result either of carelessness on the part of the IRA or of good police work by the Special Branch, but was due to treachery by old hands within the IRA itself. The blame appeared to devolve on the Chief of Staff, Stephen Hayes, who was arrested at a routine IRA meeting in Dublin on 30 June 1941. He was taken – with his brother-in-law Larry de Lacey, also of Enniscorthy, Co. Wicklow – and imprisoned in an isolated cottage in the Wicklow mountains. Larry de Lacey escaped from this cottage, but Hayes was taken to a house in Rathmines. Court-martialled there on 23 July, he was found guilty of conspiring with 'The Irish Free State Government' to obstruct the policy and impede the progress of the IRA, and of treachery 'for having deliberately forwarded information of a secret and confidential nature concerning the activities of the Irish Republican Army to a hostile body, to wit, the Irish Free State Government', and sentenced to death.

According to the IRA account of the affair, Hayes then expressed a wish to write a confession in which he admitted his involvement with the Government authorities, a task which occupied his attention until 8 September, the day he was due to be shot. However, during the early morning of that day, he found himself alone in a room with an IRA man called Liam Burke who was writing a letter and had somewhat incautiously left his revolver and holster hanging by the mantelpiece. Hayes grabbed the revolver, flung himself out of the window and shuffled away down Castlewood Avenue, his legs still shackled, to Rathmines Garda station.

In this alleged confession Hayes claimed, among other things, that he had arranged the Coventry bomb explosion in 1939 and other explosions in Britain to discredit the IRA.

If Hayes had been working for the Government – which they strenuously denied – they chose a strange way of rewarding him: on 19 June 1942 he was sentenced to five years' imprisonment for maintaining an illegal armed force. Incidentally, his brother-in-law, Larry de Lacey, worked as a sub in the *Irish Times*. I happened to find his loaded revolver in the subs' lavatory one night; as I came out holding this terrifying object at arm's length, Larry took it from me very quietly and slipped it into the back pocket of his pants without a word. So much for the professionalism of the IRA of the period. Nobody else in the room – and there were five or six subs present – paid a blind bit of attention.

Before leaving the year 1941, it is perhaps worth noting a few events of interest which were not subject to press censorship and were reported at the time. James Joyce died in Zurich on 13 January, 1941, aged 58; the *Irish Independent* described him as having 'reviled the religion in which he had been brought up and fouled the nest which was his native city'. Then in September, Davy Byrne's 'moral' pub in Duke Street, Dublin – the one featured in *Ulysses*, from which the annual Bloomsday Pilgrimage starts out every 16 June – was sold and turned into a fashionable cocktail bar, catering for the smart set. The Clondalkin Paper Mills bought 8,000 tons of straw from the year's bumper harvest to use instead of wood pulp for paper manufacture, and the Dublin Gaiety Theatre celebrated its 70th anniversary with a performance by the Hilton Edwards–Michael MacLiammoir Theatre Company of Shaw's *Caesar and Cleopatra*, and a poem specially written for the occasion by John Betjeman, press attaché to Sir John Maffey, the British Representative, and read by Anew McMaster. On 2

December, a drifting mine hit the Tuskar Rock off the coast of Wexford, killing the lighthouse-keeper, Patrick Scanlon.

By 1942 I had become a reporter, normally assigned to events as dull as the monthly meeting of a Dublin charity known as the Sick and Indigent Roomkeepers' Society – and by us reporters as 'the Sick and Indignant Roomkeepers' Society' – and the weekly luncheon of the Dublin Rotary Club where the normally extremely boring speeches were in some slight measure relieved by the fact that the Club always offered the 'gentlemen of the press' a free bottle of Guinness or beer to drink with their lunch. I also remember covering a ploughing championship – horses only, naturally – and a court case in which a Dublin man called Ernest Singleton was awarded £2,500 damages against Nestor Johnston, a student, who had seduced his daughter. The judge, a Mr Justice Hanna, remarked that it was a very serious offence to take advantage of an unmarried girl, and added darkly: 'particularly by people of the black races'.

10

The Two Armies

Of the two armies which had been in existence in Ireland at the outbreak of war, the regular Army went from strength to strength, but the IRA, for all practical purposes, ceased for a long time to exist as an organised force after the Hayes 'confession' was released.

It was Sean McCaughey, described as Adjutant-General of the IRA, who had extracted Hayes's 150-page 'confession' from him – or according to some accounts of the affair, had actually dictated part or all of it. He had been sentenced to death on 18 September 1941 by the Special Criminal Court, but this sentence was commuted to one of penal servitude for life on 25 September. He was imprisoned in the maximum security jail at Portlaoighise, and when he refused to wear convict uniform – IRA prisoners in the Curragh, Arbour Hill and Mountjoy Prison were all permitted to wear their own clothes – he was put in solitary confinement. He would wear nothing other than his prison blanket, and was allowed neither visitors nor any outdoor exercise whatever for almost five years until his death in May 1946, after twenty-two days on hunger strike and seventeen days on hunger-and-thirst strike. When questioned at the inquest about the fact that McCaughey had never been allowed any exercise, the prison governor, Major Barrows, replied: 'Decency forbade it, and apart from that, his health would not stand it. You cannot have a naked man walking about a prison.' The irony of his concern over the health of a man whose inquest he was attending seems to have escaped the Major.

Pearse Kelly – subsequently a colleague of mine when, after The Emergency, he joined the *Irish Press* as a reporter – had been one of Hayes's captors. He now decided to circulate Hayes's 'confession' to a number of Dail deputies, senators, bishops and other VIPs (whose addresses he and his IRA companions got from a copy of *Thom's Directory*) with disastrous results.

Until this document appeared, the vast majority of the IRA were quite unaware that Hayes had even been kidnapped, and as Tim Pat Coogan puts it in his book on the IRA, 'this confession of deceit and treachery dismayed them'. He goes on to add that Tarlach O'hUid, one of the top Ulster IRA men, summed up the general IRA reaction when he commented:

As far as I was concerned, the confession meant

the end of the IRA for me. There I was in Derry Jail, already fed up to the back teeth with my comrades, and the circumstances which had led me here, and this thing came. To me it meant either that Hayes was a traitor, in which case the IRA was a lousy organisation for having such a man at the top, or else that he was innocent, in which case the IRA was a doubly lousy organisation to extract such a document from him.

One of the unsolved crimes mentioned in Hayes's 'confession' concerned a Michael Devereux of Wexford, a battalion officer in the IRA who, according to his family, had simply 'gone out for a drive' one evening in 1940 and never returned, though the burnt-out wreckage of his car had been found in the Knockmealdown mountains in Co. Waterford. According to the 'confession', he had been tried by the IRA *in absentia*, found guilty of spying for the police, and shot by order of the divisional IRA commanding officer of the Wexford area. Following the release of the 'confession', detectives masquerading as IRA men from headquarters conned a local IRA man into leading them to a cave in the Knockmealdown mountains where they found Devereux's body.

Two men, Joseph O'Connor and George Plant, were arrested and charged with the murder of Michael Devereux. The evidence against them included statements which amounted to confessions from two former IRA men, Patrick Davern and Michael Walsh, who had also been involved in the Devereux affair.

Under very heavy pressure from the IRA, they re-
tracted their evidence during the O'Connor-Plant
trial, which they were legally entitled to do at that
time. O'Connor and Plant were acquitted, and then
rearrested as members of an illegal organisation as
they were leaving the court.

The Government reacted sharply by immediately
changing the law, bringing in a new Emergency Powers Order (No. 139) which provided that, whether
an offence had been committed before or after this
particular order was made, so long as it was proved
that a statement relevant to the charge had been made
by any person, including the accused, and that such a
statement had been made voluntarily, taken down in
writing and acknowledged (signed) lawfully, 'then at
any stage of the trial the prosecution may read such
a statement as evidence'.

The Order further provided that if a military court
considered it proper on any occasion during a trial
that it should not be bound by any rule of evidence,
whether of military or of common law, then the court
should not be bound by such rule.

With legislation like this ranged against them, how
could the IRA possibly have survived?

The passing of this legislation did not go unnoticed, despite the rigorous press censorship. The
Irish Times's legal correspondent attacked the new
Emergency Powers Order which, as he said, allowed
unsupported statements by witnesses to be admitted
as evidence against a prisoner, and made it possible
for a military court to inflict the death penalty on

the basis of evidence from a witness who did not even have to appear before the court; he described this as 'the abolition of trial', and the Labour Party tried unsuccessfully to have the Order annulled.

In the High Court on 13 January 1942, a habeas corpus order was requested in relation to the men charged with the Devereux murder, and an order was also requested to prohibit the military court from proceeding with the trial; these were refused three days later and subsequently, on 27 January, after an appeal, they were again refused by the Supreme Court. In the Dail that day, Mr de Valera said that trial by jury was no longer capable of safeguarding the interests of the community, and it was extremely difficult to get people to give evidence at all. He admitted that there was a danger in the admissibility of documents the author of which was not before the court investigating the crime, but argued that in the special circumstances the body investigating a crime should have the power to consider evidence that the British rule of law would not admit.

The Labour motion to annul Emergency Powers Order No. 139 was defeated in the Dail on 29 January 1942 by 71 votes to 20. Sean MacEntee said that the order was directed at 'an organisation controlled by desperate, unscrupulous and blood-hardened men . . . I cannot conceive that in the whole of its history this nation has ever confronted a greater peril. Any conspiracy designed to embroil the people in war is a grave menace to the state.'

The second Devereux murder trial opened at the

Special Criminal Court, the military tribunal sitting in Collins Barracks, on 12 February 1942. George Plant of Tipperary and Joseph O'Connor (alias O'Donnell) of Co. Kerry were again charged with the murder of Michael Devereux, believed to be a police spy, in September 1940. In the dock with them, also charged with involvement in the murder, were Michael Walsh of Kilkenny and Patrick Davern of Co. Wexford, the two men who had withdrawn their statements during the course of the first trial.

On 26 February, three of them – Plant, Davern and Walsh – were sentenced to death by firing squad. O'Connor was acquitted and then rearrested as he left the court, and taken into custody; he spent the remainder of The Emergency interned in the Curragh. Later the death sentences on Walsh and Davern were commuted to terms of imprisonment, but Plant was executed in Portlaoighise Jail on 5 March 1942.

On 4 April 1942, Liam Rice, who had been shot in the shoulder in a gun duel with detectives at Castlewood Park, Rathmines on the day Stephen Hayes escaped from the IRA and gave himself up, was sentenced to 20 years' penal servitude for shooting at a policeman, and on 19 June, Stephen Hayes himself was found guilty by the Special Criminal Court of having usurped a function of Government by maintaining an armed force and of being a member of an illegal organisation. Convicted under Emergency Powers Order No. 139, on evidence contained in a letter written by himself, he was sentenced to five years' penal servitude.

By now, all the leading lights in the IRA were dead, or in prison, and most of the rank and file were interned in the Curragh Military Camp for the duration of The Emergency. Any members of the organisation lucky enough to have escaped the attention of the authorities so far very wisely decided from then on to keep their heads down and their mouths shut . . . with one exception, which we'll come to later.

The ramshackle old army camp on the Curragh, known as Tintown, was where IRA men who had not been tried for any crime were interned as members of an illegal organisation. If additional punishment was required, there was always the notorious Glasshouse, which was also used to house members of the regular armed forces in need of corrective treatment.

The first intake of internees had arrived at the Curragh early in 1940, in the course of the police and military sweep which had come in the wake of the Magazine Fort raid. Finding themselves in a dreary cordoned-off settlement of low wooden huts, furnished only with beds and surrounded by muddy fields and barbed wire, and with nothing to do all day, the Republican prisoners amused themselves by causing as much trouble as possible for their gaolers. In December 1940, they set fire to a few selected buildings, but a strong wind spread the flames and did a lot more damage than had originally been intended. Retribution was swift: the suspected ringleaders were forced to run the gauntlet between two lines of soldiers all the way to the 'Glasshouse', and were badly bruised and beaten by the time they arrived. The rest of the internees were locked in the remaining huts from Saturday evening until Monday morning, and when they were allowed out on the Monday morning and lined up for breakfast, some soldiers fired into the line of internees and injured six men, one fatally. At the inquest Sean McBride was only permitted to ask one question: 'Why was Barney Casey shot in the back?'

In an article in the *Irish Times* Supplement of 8 May 1985, about The Emergency, J. Bowyer Bell, author of *The Secret Army: the IRA 1916–1979* wrote:

The inquest was adjourned at once. The government wanted no scandal, no incidents out on the Curragh from those pieces removed from the board. And there was no 'scandal' then or later, Tintown and The Glasshouse could have been in another country for all the Irish public knew or cared, as the nation moved into the second year of The Emergency . . . From the outside there was no good news, only rumours of arrests, North and South. The internees were no longer waiting out a 'campaign' – the English bombs no longer detonated – or serving as silent witnesses for a just cause. They were in the main simply waiting . . . whatever the affront to democratic rights, Tintown and the Glasshouse performed as required, transformed the IRA militants into bored internees, squabbling

over carrying coal, memorising Irish verbs, waiting on other, distant events. Life passed them
by. Careers aborted. Fiancées found other men.
Families struggled along without them. Children
grew up into strangers . . . Dev and the State had
prevailed.

The Curragh Camp was also the principal camp for
the regular army, which had reached full strength by
1942. In the period following the invasion of the Low
Countries and the fall of France, the Government had
created a new category of regular soldier, the Emergency Durationist – or the E-men who signed on for
the duration of The Emergency – and the addition of
these new recruits raised the army strength to nearly
40,000, more men than could be comfortably housed,
fed and equipped in fact.

Equipment was a major problem. Plans to set up
a small armaments factory in Ireland had to be dropped when war broke out. All that the army could
boast of in the way of panzer divisions were thirteen Rolls-Royce light armoured cars at least twenty
years old, and armed with Vickers .303 machine
guns, plus a dozen Swedish light armoured cars
and four similar vehicles manufactured in Ireland
on a Leyland chassis. During The Emergency, a few
more armoured cars were produced in Ireland, some
at the Great Southern Railway Works at Inchicore
and others built by Thomas Thompson & Co. of
Carlow. There were cycle squadrons – known as 'the
Piddling Panzers', manned by young men who had

learned to cycle in the cycling clubs and in *An Oige*, Ireland's Youth Hostel movement – and motor-cycle squadrons, and arms enough to go round. In the end, the energetic and systematic search for arms after the Magazine Fort Raid had produced far more arms and ammunition than had ever seen the inside of the Fort.

The new Marine Service, and the part-time Maritime Inscription – very largely manned by yacht owners and their crews – now had six fast motor-torpedo-boats acquired from Britain, and miscellaneous small craft for mine-laying and training, including a handsome 132-ton Cork schooner, as well as the *Muirchu* and another fisheries protection vessel, the *Fort Rannoch*. In addition to the six new Lysanders, the Air Corps had Gloster Gladiators, Avro Ansons and a couple of Walrus Amphibians. Their rifles, bayonets, revolvers, machine-guns and gas-masks were all vintage First World War types, and the pilots still wore Biggles-style leather helmets with goggles, as some of the planes had open cockpits.

British planes were constantly crashing or crash-landing on Irish territory during the war, and at one stage the Air Corps was in a position to offer the British a mixed bag of two Mark I Hurricanes in good condition; a damaged Spitfire, Martlet and Beaufighter; two wrecked Spitfires, for spares; and three tons of scrap from three Blenheim bombers, one Wellington bomber and one Lockheed Hudson in return for four Mark II Hurricanes, which they eventually got, with a little cash adjustment.

The biggest problem of all, so far as the army was concerned, was accommodation; the existing barracks, almost all inherited from the British, were inadequate and old-fashioned, a number of derelict or near-derelict big houses, castles and the few old RIC barracks which had not been burnt down or blown up during The Troubles were taken over and refurbished for army use. In general, apart from oil and petrol, the army provided their own fuel; there was a Construction Corps, composed mainly of young unemployed men aged 17–25, whose tasks officially included road construction, aerodrome maintenance, forestry and turf-cutting, though men from all branches of the armed forces volunteered to help with the turf harvest. In 1942, another army was recruited, *Sluagh na Talmhan*, an Irish land army, to help with the harvest; but by harvest time, it could boast no more than 320 volunteers.

Then there was the Local Defence Force. The original LSF (Local Security Force), referred to earlier, had numbered 148,000-odd at the height of the recruiting drive, but the flimsy brown denim overalls with which they were issued as a uniform, the shortage of equipment, and particularly of arms, had led to a falling-off in numbers and by 1941 its strength was down to about 100,000, largely unarmed. According to John Bowman in *De Valera and the Ulster Question 1917–1973* (Oxford University Press, 1982) this was a situation not entirely unsatisfactory to de Valera since there were some, at least, of the new recruits whom he did not wish to arm. 'They were,' Bowman goes on, 'apparently safer in uniform than not, but safer still without weapons – a point which well indicates the peculiar subtleties of de Valera's dilemma at this particular time.'

From the beginning of 1941, the LSF 'A' Group became the LDF, the Local Defence Force, in new green uniforms, under the direct control of the army; the LSF 'B' Group, wearing blue uniforms, worked with the police on traffic control, communications, ARP and other protective duties as well as operating night patrols to watch out for parachutists.

By 1942, the LDF had settled down and started to train in earnest, pleased with their new uniforms but still sadly lacking in arms and other equipment. My own commanding officer, T.F. O'Higgins, by now a TD, had raised the matter in the Dail on 3 March 1941: 'We have 100,000 LDF men with empty hands,' he said. 'And we have 20,000 LDF men with rifles of a bore that limits the supply of ammunition to . . . about a couple of hours [active] service.'

Whether the Irish armed forces could have held an invading force at bay for more than a few hours at best is debatable – the maximum army strength never rose beyond two divisions, and in the battle for the Low Countries the Germans disposed of 156 divisions – but the point is that between the army, the LDF, the LSF, the Army Air Corps and the Marine Service there was a total of about 250,000 well-trained, well-disciplined men and women prepared to stand up and face anybody who attempted to invade neutral Ireland.

*   *   *

On 26 January 1942, several thousand US combat troops arrived in Northern Ireland. On the following day, de Valera stated that the Irish Government had not been consulted by either the British Government or the American Government about the arrival of these troops. When told of de Valera's reaction to the arrival of the GIs by an American newsman, President Roosevelt's reply consisted of one word: 'Really?' he said.

Although Lemass had frequently made veiled references to the possibility of rationing, and on 7 January had announced a general rationing scheme, nobody knew when or even whether it was going to happen. I found out on 22 March, the first and only scoop of my entire journalistic career, which came about in this way.

One day when I was reporting the Dail, I noticed that some of the usual paperwork – the list of questions for the Ministers, the order paper, or the previous day's *Iris Oifiguil* (the Irish *Hansard*), I forget which – was missing, and in the office next day I chanced to mention this fact to Matt Chambers, then deputy Chief Reporter.

'Why don't you ring Cahills and find out what went wrong?' Matt suggested. Cahills of Parkgate Street was the biggest printing and publishing firm in Dublin and printed all the Government papers as well as the *English Digest*, the *Irish Digest*, *The Bell* magazine and a wide range of paperback books including all the Zane Grey westerns.

I rang Cahill's and asked why the previous day's

order papers had not been ready in time for the Dail sitting. I didn't even say who I was. I didn't have to; the man who chanced to answer the phone was only too anxious to spread the news.

'Ah, well, now d'you see, we've been that busy printing the ration books before the start of May that we've got a bit behind in some of our other work.'

And that was it. The next day the *Irish Times* was the first – and only – paper to print the fact that 3,000,000 ration books were now printed and ready for distribution; rationing would begin in May.

And it did. The ration books went out on 6 May, but told us nothing since they consisted solely of pages of different coloured numbered coupons, but on 8 May Lemass revealed some of the details in a broadcast to the nation. The biggest shock was the clothes ration: 40 coupons for a man's suit out of a total allowance of 52 for a year, but almost immediately increased (after determined and noisy protests from the Dublin drapers) to 78 for a year. In July, the Department of Industry and Commerce warned the public of an impending paper shortage, partly due to the amount of paper used to print nearly three million ration books. No newsprint had been imported since the spring of 1941, and the *Irish Times* had already suggested that its readers should adopt the habit of sharing their copy with a neighbour or friend.

Apart from the continuing shortage of fuel, another big worry was grain. In February, Lemass broadcast an appeal for self-denial in the consumption of bread and announced that in future it would be made from 100 per cent wheat flour, which would mean a much darker loaf. A new 'flour controller' was appointed and flour retailers and hotels were asked to try to ensure a fair distribution. The *Irish Times* sponsored a 'No Bread for Breakfast' League, which was known as the NBBL and quickly came to be called Nibble; the *Irish Times* printed badges to be worn by NBBL members – these were much in evidence in Leinster House – and the artist Sean Keating designed a Nibble poster, urging people to join the League. By April it was clear that bread would have to be rationed; an allowance of 7 oz per person per day was predicted, and in May it was made illegal to serve bread or wheaten flour in any form at dances, race-meetings, whist or bridge drives, bazaars, carnivals or sales of work.

The arrival of a cargo of wheat on 28 May ensured a ration of 3½ lbs per person per week for another eight weeks only, but no more. Early in the year the malting of barley had been suspended to allow the Government to examine its impact on the cereal situation, and for a time it looked as if beer and stout might have to be rationed, an unthinkable disaster. Daniel Twomey, Secretary of the Department of Agriculture, warned the Dail that the position as regards wheat was so critical that Ireland might have to produce its full requirement of wheat or go without bread altogether. Sugar was also scarce. In June, Lemass told the Dail that there were only 45,000 acres under sugar beet in 1942, as against

73,000 in 1941; this was entirely due to the shortage of artificial fertiliser.

Fuel continued to be the most serious shortage because it affected the distribution of all the other scarce commodities. There was now enough turf stacked along the New Bog Road in Phoenix Park to meet the immediate needs of Dublin's 500,000 inhabitants, but in order to provide for the future, 29 new wooden canal barges had been ordered; these would be propelled by genuine horse-power and the locks on the Grand Canal would be operated round the clock. A boom town – 20 miles long, between Edenderry, Co. Offaly and Newbridge, Co. Kildare, and consisting of a ribbon development of portakabins and temporary dwellings of all sorts – had grown up along the road through the Bog of Allen to accommodate the army of turf-cutters employed winning turf for Dublin's fires in the winter of 1942–43.

By this time, too, many Dubliners had bought or rented tracts of turf bog in the Dublin Mountains, and were spending the weekends winning their own turf. Other Dubliners had rented plots to help the shortage situation by growing their own food. And when the plots in Phoenix Park were ravaged by the famous Phoenix Park herds of deer, repeated protests by 400 plot-holders forced the Dublin Corporation to introduce a programme of culling for the first time, and many Dubliners had their first taste of venison.

Hugo Flinn, the Turf Controller, announced in May that experienced agricultural and turf workers would not be permitted to leave the country until the harvest was in. Two sacks of coal had been allowed per household, along with two tons of turf, for the months of February and March. But on 30 March it was announced that there would be no more coal for domestic use; imports were barely enough to keep industry going.

The calorific value of Dublin's gas was reduced again and again. In February, the Gas Company warned the Government that it did not propose to lay gas-pipes or fit gas-stoves in any new houses being built, and on 2 March gas was rationed in Dublin by the system earlier used elsewhere in Ireland; it was available only for short periods during the day, which were further reduced on 14 May to three periods: 5.30–9.0 a.m., 11.30 a.m.–1.30 p.m. and 6–7 p.m. In May, too, the ESB (Electricity Supply Board) took power to ration electricity and cut off defaulters from all supplies; the Board wanted a total prohibition of space heating, and cuts of 50 per cent of electricity used for water heating, 25 per cent used for lighting and 10 per cent used as motive power.

On 9 March, the *Irish Times* announced that 'Motoring was on its last tyres'. No further provision would be made by tyre manufacturers for motor-car tyres; these would be available only by special permit, and their manufacture was being restricted to those used by heavy goods vehicles, vans and lorries. The manufacture of rubber footwear, golf and tennis balls, hot-water bottles and all other such articles made from crude rubber had been forbidden by Government Order from January.

On 16 March, petrol for private cars for April was cut to half the existing rate, and would cease altogether at the end of that month. Private cars fitted with producer-gas units would not be put off the roads, but they would receive no petrol, no tyres and no guarantee of supplies of fuel for making the gas.

By April, there was a 10 p.m. curfew for all buses and considerable reductions in all road transport services; on 9 April, Sean Lemass again talked to the nation on the radio. 'All non-essential travelling by road services is to stop by tonight,' he said, 'Not tomorrow. Only thus can you ensure the delivery of necessities to your homes.' He added that when current stocks of rubber ran out there would be no lorries to carry turf, beet or wheat. Irish race-meetings were cut by half, the use of motor transport for race-meetings forbidden, and rail transport not guaranteed. Rail transport was still suffering badly from being obliged to use a mixture of turf, wood and slack instead of best coal; one train from Broadstone Station in Dublin to Athlone was passed twice by the same canal barge, after being forced to stop to relight the firebox, and in the winter of 1942, it took a passenger train 23 hours to cover the 210 miles between Killarney and Dublin. 'Here she comes! Right on the day!' exulted a railway porter in a *Dublin Opinion* cartoon.

When the ESB warned that water-power alone could not provide electricity for more than the next few months, tramway services were severely curtailed. By now motoring was limited to Ministers of State, leaders of the Opposition, Government and local authority officials, Dail deputies and senators who lived in the country, representatives of foreign countries, clergymen, doctors, vets and midwives. Many doctors, vets and midwives now did their rounds on push bicycles.

In Co. Limerick, Lord Adare provided a stage-coach service between Limerick Railway Station and his home at Adare, now a luxury hotel, using a four-horse stage-coach he had managed to find in Liverpool, which could accommodate 20 passengers, inside and out. Another stage-coach service replaced the bus services between Howth, Baldoyle and Malahide, Lucan and Bray, using 18-seater coaches and, again, teams of four horses. A number of old Dublin horse-drawn cabs had been refurbished and were supplementing the services of the fast disappearing taxis. Side-cars (popularly known as 'jaunting' cars) reappeared outside Galway Railway Station to transport tourists to Salthill, the popular seaside resort on Galway Bay.

Experiments to solve Ireland's immediate problems continued. At one stage it was thought that if the carbon dioxide produced during the brewing of Guinness stout were tapped off and compressed in cylinders by IFS (Industrial Gases) Ltd, it could provide enough gas for the country's needs from the waste products of the brewery; but, probably because of the shortage of other ingredients necessary to carry out the process, the experiments fell through and nothing came of the idea. In July, there was a story in the newspapers that Irish tobacco-growers aimed to contribute 240,000 lbs of home-grown tobacco to the million pounds of the weed annually smoked in Ireland, but nothing much seems to have come of that either. A new company, Waste Paper Ltd, was formed to collect waste paper for recycling, as earlier attempts to encourage children to do this for 6d a bundle had not proved very successful.

The Hammond Lane Foundry produced a domestic range specifically designed to burn turf. Solas Teoranta, the firm set up to manufacture electric light bulbs for Ireland, not only used sand from a Donegal beach to produce the glass, but also heat made from a producer-gas unit burning turf. A Captain McGoldrick of the Curragh Camp invented a turf-cutting machine which could cut a slab of turf containing approximately 80 sods out of the bog in one movement; it could be operated by six men or one horse. The Government reopened the Wicklow mines at Avoca and formed a state-sponsored company, the Minerals (Exploration and Development) Co. to mine iron pyrites and produce sulphuric acid.

On the food front, macon – a word coined to describe mutton – cured like bacon and sliced into rashers – went on sale in the summer, but the macon rashers did not prove very popular with the public.

The Dail voted £365,000 to provide compensation and other payments for damage to property due to the dropping of bombs by foreign aircraft. By spring 1942, shelters had been built to accommodate 32,900 people and work had started on a further 600 shelters for another 30,000 people; unnecessarily, as it turned out, for no further bombs fell on Irish territory. In the Dail, J.M. Dillon (Fine Gael), who had resolutely opposed Ireland's neutrality from the beginning of the war, said on 10 February:

> Whoever attacks America is my enemy without reservation or qualification, and I say that the US has been treacherously and feloniously attacked by Germany, Italy and Japan. Those nations are therefore my enemies and I would to God that they were the enemies of a united Irish people.

A little less than a week later, he resigned from the Fine Gael Party, but continued to sit in the Dail as an Independent.

At Trim Circuit Criminal Court in Meath, in February, the Rev. Francis Moran, parish priest of Castletown, was charged with causing the death of William Ryan, a farm labourer, by striking him with his hand at Walkinstown on 14 January, while the labourer was denying a charge of immorality. Not only was the priest released on his own bail of £100, but when he was tried on 20 April he was found not guilty of manslaughter. Also in February, the Lenten Pastorals warned against the growing laxity of conscience and the development of a new paganism, 'concomitants of the conflict from which Ireland had been miraculously preserved'. Although the bishops were not referring to ordinary crime, there had in fact been an alarming increase in theft, housebreaking and burglary. Gerry Boland, Minister for Justice, when telling the Dail in May that crime had doubled in Dublin since the start of The Emergency, added that commodities were being stolen by people who had never in their lives stolen anything before, but were tempted to do so because of the wartime shortages.

Despite the huge number of Irish men and women who had joined the British and Irish armed forces, or had gone to work in factories in the United Kingdom, unemployment remained surprisingly high; William Norton, the Labour leader, put the figure at 96,000 in May 1941 – a year in which 50,821 Eire citizens received permits to work in Britain and Irish emigrants in the UK sent back £2,600,000 in remittance money.

The nationalisation of public transport in Ireland was foreshadowed by an announcement in February that, for the remainder of The Emergency at least, all rail transport would come under a transport executive with plenary powers: the first chairman of the Government Board appointed to run the railways was A.P. Reynolds, managing director of the DUTC (Dublin United Tramways Company) at a salary (£2,500 a year) a good deal higher than that paid to the Taoiseach, Mr de Valera.

By now Brendan Behan had returned to Dublin after his spell in Borstal and on April 24, at the age of 17, he was sentenced to 14 years' imprisonment for taking part in a shooting affray on the Finglas Road on Easter Monday. It was that generation of the IRA's last dying kick.

But the IRA, as the British authorities have discovered

to their surprise and frequent discomfiture, is an organisation that is, it seems, eternally self-perpetuating, in countless different forms and breakaway movements like the Provos, the INLA and now the Irish Continuity Council.

11

❧❧❧❧

STRANGE ARRIVISTES

By the beginning of 1943, the Irish people were becoming accustomed to burning turf, travelling by bicycle and making do on meagre rations of very unappetising but extremely healthy bread. The danger of invasion by either Britain or Germany now seemed to have faded, and although a great many things were very scarce – tea particularly – nobody had died of starvation yet, and it was beginning to look as if the Irish might even be able to hold out until the end of the war, which now seemed to be vaguely in sight. The Battle of El Alamein had been fought and won, and the Allies were advancing across the North African coast towards the toe of Italy, while the British and American forces – in Britain and in Northern Ireland – were clearly preparing to launch a 'Second Front' invasion of Europe.

Public and private transport was on its very last legs. Since coal provided the electricity for Dublin's trams, tram services had been drastically curtailed from 1942 and were suspended completely from 1944 – and, in fact, never returned.

As Bernard Share remarked in an earlier book about the period, *The Emergency: Neutral Ireland 1939–45* (Dublin: Gill & Macmillan, 1978):

> It was a quiet land. The internal combustion engine had been virtually banished from the roads. The petrol ration for those engaged on essential services was miserly (for the ordinary citizen it was non-existent) and any abuse could lead to its immediate withdrawal . . . a taxi-driver would lose his permit if he carried his fares even to the proximity of a race-course, if races were being run. Starters and racing officials were, however, allowed to proceed to race meet-ings in taxis [the Government didn't want to kill off one of its own golden geese altogether], but not trainers, jockeys nor bookmakers, a nice distinction which drew the inevitable protests . . . From April 1942, it became illegal for owners of motor vehicles to have gas producer plants fitted to them, unless they could satisfy the government that the vehicle was being used for essential services. From April 30, 1944, the petrol ration – tiny as it was – was withdrawn even from doctors and clergymen living in the city.

However, many people used cycles, even for relatively lengthy journeys from Dublin to Galway for the purpose of attending the Galway Races. Paddy Campbell was one such when writing the *Irishman's Diary*, in 1944.

This is what cycling one hundred and thirty-two miles is like. When the cyclist starts he looks like an advertisement for the all-steel model. You know that special cheery holiday wave, the neat roll of luggage on the back, and the beaming smile. The cyclist is smiling and waving because he is off to the open road, self-confident, bronzed and fit.

Thirty miles on, the cyclist looks like the last refugee out of Paris, one hand supporting his back, the other laid on the handle-bars. He can in fact scarcely reach the handle-bars with the agonising pain that is burning along his spine.

Another thirty miles and the cyclist is collapsed over the cross-bar. He can no longer support his spine vertically. His head droops between his shoulders. His face is lined and spotted with dead insects. He is having saddle trouble, and shifts backwards and forwards, seeking relief.

But the strange thing is that the cyclist is now moving like the wind. This is because the senses have left his legs. He watches the knees rise and fall with no knowledge that they are his . . .

Dublin at this period understandably attracted numerous strange types; conscientious objectors, draft-dodgers, spivs of all kinds, rich people anxious to rent property in Ireland to escape the bombs, others who were hoping to find a nirvana into which they could import their Bentleys and run them, perhaps, on the producer gas made from turf and wood which they had been reading about in the British newspapers. Obviously, they had not heard that new producer-gas units had now suddenly been banned.

Most of the new arrivals in Dublin seemed to have plenty of money to spend, and it is the recollection of the majority of my contemporaries who remained in Dublin during The Emergency that it eventually turned into one long, lovely bender. There were parties every night of the week and horse-races and yacht regattas most weekends during the sailing season, as well as almost continuous tennis parties, and all the pubs were crowded most of the time. Among the visitors were many Unionists from the Six Counties; dour, hard-faced men who had been earning good money in the shipyards and aircraft and armament factories of Northern Ireland and who had come down south, their pockets bulging with money, in search of steaks and stout and a good time, leaving a lot of their Puritan prejudices behind them.

Also among the visitors were countless young Irish men and women on leave from the armed forces. Brian Inglis, who had left the *Irish Times* in 1939 to join the RAF, was a frequent visitor; on one occasion he crossed the border from Eglinton Airfield on Lough

Foyle to attend the annual press and advertising golf tournament at Bundoran, and he kept turning up in Dublin. 'There was no sensation of going to an ideologically-different country,' he remembered, adding: 'It was as if the Allies had voluntarily set apart a region where steaks and drink and bright lights were provided – a kind of convalescent home.'

Inglis also recalled an occasion when he had a few drinks with his ex-editor, R.M. Smyllie, and Karl Petersen, the German press attaché in Dublin: 'To have exchanged casual pub conversation with a citizen of a country which I was engaged in fighting would, I thought, make a good story to tell when I got back to the mess.'

We had visitors like Beverly Nichols, then at the height of his fame as a popular Fleet Street daily columnist and an extremely prolific writer on subjects he considered might prove sensational, like his ill-considered and hysterical diatribe against war, *Cry Havoc*. He was the only Fleet Street columnist who had the audacity to write his autobiography at the age of 25 and call it just that: *Twenty-five*. I remember interviewing him in his suite in the Shelbourne Hotel, where he sat at a baby-grand piano, a white silk scarf loosely knotted around his throat, strumming excerpts from compositions of his own, mostly thin imitations of Noël Coward's music, and complaining that he had been invited by the Palace Bar crowd to accompany them on the annual Boyne Walk, held in memory of the poet F.R. Higgins who had died a couple of years earlier. And what had happened? Having sat waiting for them in the Shelbourne foyer from 10 o'clock in the morning, dressed in a Donegal tweed suit and stout walking shoes, he had then returned after an excellent lunch to continue waiting all afternoon, still dressed for an encounter with the rugged Irish countryside. Not long after he had eventually retired to his suite in the late afternoon, a straggle of them arrived just as it was getting dark and announced that the Walk was off for this year. 'Owing to the inclement weather,' one of them explained to him, 'it has taken so much time to get from the Palace Bar to the Shelbourne, that it wouldn't be wise to attempt the Boyne Walk this year.' They had then agreed to have one final one for the road, all round, on him, after which they disappeared without suggesting any further meetings.

Some extremely odd oddballs turned up, among them a once-famous Irish boxer who had won a number of prize-fights in the States before going to seed in Hollywood. Jack Doyle was well known under his pseudonym, 'The Gorgeous Gael', and on arrival in Ireland with a minor Mexican film actress known as Movita, he announced his willingness to join the Irish armed forces if called upon to do so. In the meantime, he married Movita in Westland Row Catholic Church in Dublin on 11 February 1943, and on 11 June 1943 resumed his career as a boxer by being thoroughly beaten in the first round by an Irish heavyweight in the course of his first appearance in the ring in Dalymount Park, Dublin. Before long, his marriage was on the rocks and the only opponent he was knocking out regularly was the unfortunate Movita, a situation which soon resulted in a tumultuous divorce.

Other visitors to Dublin at this time included Laurence Olivier, who arrived on 28 March, looking for locations for a film he was planning to make based on Shakespeare's *Henry V*. He found his perfect Agincourt in the demenses of Lord Powerscourt at Enniskerry, Co. Wicklow, and his film was such a success that Ireland soon became extremely popular with film producers and their crews, not only for the juicy steaks, oysters, crabs, prawns and fresh salmon (and in those days they were all wild salmon in Ireland, for salmon farming didn't begin in Ireland until after the war) that were still available for people with enough money to pay for them, but also because Eire – then still largely an undeveloped country – could provide locations mercifully free of electric pylons, skyscraper tower blocks, motor traffic, elaborate road junctions, barrage balloons, aircraft in the skies and so many of the other appurtenances of so-called civilisation, and consequently could be disguised as anywhere else, at any other period of time.

Among the miscellaneous arrivals during this period were a number of modern artists and avant-garde poets, mostly English and headed by a painter/poet called Nick Nicholls and a middle-European called Basil Rakowski, who formed a movement known as the White Stag Group. They lived and drank and held their exhibitions in the Baggot Street area, which became the centre of yet another Dublin Left

Bank society, and before long these immigrants were joined by the very few modern artists in Dublin, among them Jack Yeats, Mainie Jellet, Evie Hone and Louis le Brocquy, to whom their arrival gave fresh impetus to rebel against the artistic establishment.

Art in Ireland at this period was in the firm grip of what might be loosely described as the academic tradition, and its impact is probably best illustrated by the fact that when the Friends of the National Collection – an association of well-meaning and well-heeled citizens, dedicated to purchasing paintings for Ireland's galleries – went to the trouble and expense of buying Georges Rouault's 'Christ and the Soldier' for the Municipal Gallery of Modern Art, it was turned down on the grounds that it was highly blasphemous, as well as being 'naïve, childish and unintelligible'. However, the problem was solved in an unexpected and completely satisfactory way: the very civilised priests from the seminary at Maynooth, St Patrick's College, expressed themselves delighted to take the painting on loan, and there it hung in the library until public taste in Dublin changed. Today it hangs where it ought to have done from the start of the affair, in the Sir Hugh Lane Municipal Gallery of Modern Art.

Encouraged perhaps by the row over the Rouault, and by the existence in their midst of such alien, anarchistic movements as the White Stag Group, the young, breakaway Irish artists began to consider the possibilities of an Irish *Salon des Refusées*, and when some paintings by Louis Le Brocquy, a stylish if defiantly avant-garde young painter, were rejected by the Royal Hibernian Academy, help came from an unexpected quarter. As the *Irish Times* put it on 15 September 1944:

> When eighty years earlier, the Academic Painters of Paris met, it occurred to the young geniuses who were later to become internationally famous as the Impressionists that their work was not by academic standards acceptable, the Emperor Napoleon III came to the help of the *refusées* and placed a gallery at their disposal.
>
> Today, the Minister for Education, Mr T. Derring [a more enlightened man than many of his colleagues] has made a similar gesture by offering the gallery in the National College of Art for the display of work by young artists whose work is not deemed suitable for the annual exhibitions of the Royal Hibernian Academy.

This assembly of work by modern artists, known as the Irish Exhibition of Living Art, became an annual affair which after the war attracted young artists from all over the world and became the nucleus of the modern art movement in Dublin.

One of the many things that Ireland had never got around to was the provision of a central bank to handle such matters as foreign currency; in this, as in so many other matters, the new state had continued to depend on the British machinery until war broke out in 1939. In March 1942, leave was given to the Minister for Finance, Sean T. O'Kelly, to introduce a Central Bank Bill to set up an organisation which would be the principal currency authority in the state, replacing the old Currency Commission which was a relic of British rule. And in January 1943, Joseph Brennan was appointed first Governor of the new Central Bank of Ireland which had been formed to direct Eire's finances and control its currency dealings in the post-war world.

Another relic of British rule, the National Stud at Tully in Co. Kildare – started by an eccentric Englishman called Lord Wavertree at the turn of the century – became a state-sponsored company in 1943. In September, it was announced that all the activities hitherto conducted at Tully, by and on behalf of the British Government, would be transferred to Dorset in England, and that all British bloodstock at Tully was being removed to England. The lands and buildings there were duly handed over to the Irish Government in September 1943, along with a sum of £21,000 in lieu of rent dating back to 1923. The Government then decided that henceforward the stud would be run by yet another state-sponsored company, government-financed, for the benefit of the Irish bloodstock breeders, and that Irish farmers with brood mares would be allowed to draw lots for the services of the stud's top studs, so to speak, for a nominal fee, on a 'no-foal, no-fee' arrangement.

Also in 1943, long before the first stirrings of the Welfare State in Britain, de Valera announced a scheme to pay 'children's allowances' in certain circumstances. In all conscience, the amounts concerned were not all that great; 2s 6d (12½p) per week for each child under sixteen in excess of two, the payment to be made half-yearly with no means test. But it was a start, and in a country where the general attitude had always been that it was the sole and total responsibility of the father of the family to provide for all his children's needs – or not, as the case might be – it was highly revolutionary.

Also in 1943 – and long before Beeching and the passion for nationalising everything which swept Britain in the wake of the big Labour landslide victory in July 1945 – Colonel The O'Callaghan, presiding at a meeting of GSR (Great Southern Railway) stockholders in Dublin, foreshadowed the nationalisation of all road and rail transport in Ireland by announcing the nationalisation of the GSR company without compensation of any kind to the shareholders.

A general election fell due in the ordinary way in June 1943. Realising that the government in office would inevitably be blamed for everything that had recently been happening, including the disastrous outbreak of foot-and-mouth disease of 1941 and the severe shortages of fuel, tea and other commodities – matters for which the state could not have been expected to take any major responsibility – de Valera did his best to prolong the life of the Dail for one further year, but the Opposition would not hear of it. The country went to the polls on 22 June, when the combination of the petrol shortage – which drastically curtailed electioneering – and the fact that the newsprint shortage resulted in four-page papers with no room to print the usual columns of politicians' speeches, created a situation in which the electorate had no clear idea of the real issues – not indeed that they cared greatly. At this stage, de Valera had clearly been in charge of things for far too long.

Fine Gael, the main opposition party, was in favour of a national government of all parties, as in Britain, or at least a coalition of some sort. De Valera profoundly mistrusted coalition governments, since they could be held to ransom by a minority (and he knew, who better, how much damage a malevolently-minded minority could do) and it was widely rumoured that Sean MacEntee, de Valera's Minister for Local Government and Public Health, had been doing his best to scotch any notion of a coalition by telling Dublin audiences that the Muscovites were still active in Dublin, where the Communists had already kidnapped Mr William Norton, the Labour leader, and were holding him as a hostage, while the Dublin Communist Party was attempting to infiltrate the Irish Labour Party. There wasn't a word of truth in all this, but in those days any mention of Moscow was bad news in Catholic Ireland.

In the event, in the elections Fianna Fail's seats were reduced from 77 to 67, and Fine Gael's from 45 to 32. Despite MacEntee's barely credible attempts to smear them as bright red Communists, Labour did extremely well, increasing their total of seats from 9 to 17. With bad grace, de Valera managed to form another government with more or less the same ingredients, and was able to soldier on for another year, but no longer.

One of the terrible events of the same year was a fire in an orphanage run by nuns in Co. Cavan. The subsequent inquest found that 35 children lost their lives on 23 February 1943, 'although ample time existed for the rescue of all the children, if the adult children inside the convent and the voluntary workers outside [it], had had any elementary training in fire-fighting and rescue.' In the ordinary way, this would not have created such a scandal, except that in the light of Ireland's recent air-raids, people were now very well aware of what ought to be done in the event of a fire. The verdict was a direct attack on the nuns in charge of the convent, and confirmed in many people a steadily growing impression that the nuns were not really fit to look after anybody, not even themselves.

This was the infamous year when a cinema in Clones introduced regulations forcing young men and women to sit on opposite sides of the central aisle. The stricture did not apply to married persons, and marriage certificates or rings were not required to be produced, the staff of the cinema being expected to make the decision on the basis of age and general appearance. This regulation would not have mattered greatly in any other country; but in Ireland it was vital because (for reasons given earlier) virtually no opportunities for sexual contact – even of the most tenuous and unsatisfactory sort – existed outside the cinema: not in the home, nor in the dance-halls and other social amenities provided by society, nor even in the wild, assiduously monitored by the local parish priest, with the aid of binoculars if necessary.

By now Foynes, according to *The Times*, had become the busiest flying-boat junction in the world – handling, between August 1942 and July 1943, more than 1,400 aircraft and 15,000 passengers. Also in 1943, the ESB (Electricity Supply Board) announced plans for rural electrification, as soon as supplies of the necessary materials became available; the Government reckoned that complete rural electrification would cost £10,000,000.

A committee of five UCD professors, appointed to advise on what could be done to promote the Irish language in the universities, stated in a report that the average UCD student could not speak Irish and that the general attitude towards Irish was one of cynicism and dislike. Conversely, 1944 marked the jubilee of the Gaelic League; a special stamp featuring the President Dr Douglas Hyde was issued, and de Valera gave a talk to a representative selection of the women of Ireland in the Mansion House. I quote Quidnunc of *An Irishman's Diary*:

His speech began by giving thanks to the Fianna Fail workers for their part in the General Election, but quickly reverted to the Irish language, and his plan for what he called 'a Third Order of the Fainne'. This Fainne would not carry the usual obligation upon its wearer to speak nothing but Irish. It would merely be a sign that the wearer had some knowledge of the language, and was anxious to speak it, if the opportunity was offered.

Mr de Valera held out the lapel of his dinner-jacket. He said: 'I sometimes have to wear this coat on occasions when it is not possible to do without English. So I have had the Fainne embroidered on it. I asked . . .' He stopped. He was about to say 'my wife'. But then he continued, 'I asked to have the Fainne embroidered on the lapel. It is quite easy. You take the top of a fountain-pen, and dip it in . . . a powder-box.'

Mr de Valera brushed his nose with his fore-finger, smiling, the way he does when he is embarrassed. The ladies cooed. 'You then press the end of the fountain-pen cap on the lapel and it leaves a neat little circle of powder,' went on Mr de Valera. 'It is quite easy to embroider the Fainne around the circle. I think you use what I believe is called the button-hole stitch.'

By now, bombing raids on Germany were becoming increasingly frequent, and on 29 November 1943 it was learned in Dublin that the Irish Legation in Berlin had been destroyed, but that the Irish Chargé d'Affaires, William Warnock, was safe.

During the year 1943, a new problem had arisen both for the Irish Government and the government, such as it was, of the Six Counties: smuggling. The border had never been clearly marked out or policed, and people who lived in the area used the B-roads and side-roads freely. In time of war, these roads became vital for the smuggling of essential supplies backwards and forwards over the border. There had always been considerable smuggling of cattle and sheep, for the purposes of all the various subsidies, grants, exemptions etc. that were payable, even in those primitive days long before the CAP. Now a whole range of domestic commodities joined the list. For some reason, razor-blades were far more freely available in Eire than in Northern Ireland; and tea was far scarcer south of the border than in the north, so smuggling that started on this basis soon grew out of hand. For example, in 1943, a Belfast grocer was fined for 'dealing in' 137,000 razor-blades imported from Eire, and he received two months in jail for 'harbouring' 570 lbs of tea for export to Eire.

Smuggling across the border during this particular period of The Emergency included coffins packed with watches, clocks and other jewellery, because such items from neutral Switzerland, Sweden and other places – and available in Ireland – were much less plentiful in the Six Counties of Northern Ireland than in Eire, and there was more money to spend on them in Ulster. However, one man travelling the other way (from Belfast to Dublin) was arrested with 60 yds of electric cable wrapped around his body, because electrical wiring was desperately scarce in Eire from 1943 onwards. Smuggling also occurred on the railways. On some trains observed by customs officers, the fire extinguishers had been replaced by dummies which on the journey northwards from Dublin to Belfast were filled with cosmetics for the ladies (relatively plentiful in Dublin, but unobtainable in the North); while on the way south, those same dummy fire extinguishers were filled with tea, the abiding and exasperating shortage in Eire.

There was a genuine trade in British sparking plugs; the Champion L10 was the favourite with most Irish motorists, and far better than any sparking plug available in Ireland. But the term Champion L10 was also a euphemism for condoms, then unobtainable in Eire but freely available in Belfast; those were greatly in demand in Ireland during The Emergency, when for some reason (possibly not unconnected with the uncertainties occasioned by a very adjacent war) Irish girls seemed to relax their strict standards of chastity. There was considerable trade in clothing coupons too. The southern Irish received more generous clothing rations than the people from the Six Counties, but had less money to spend on clothes; and at one stage Lemass said that if the Irish people kept on selling their clothes coupons to the people from the North of Ireland, it would defeat the whole object of rationing.

So many things were smuggled across the border during The Emergency that there has to be an apocryphal tale about the trade, and here it is. At a customs post in Newry, a keen young customs officer was fazed by the number of times one young man came across the border trundling a wheelbarrow containing a sack which, on inspection, never held anything more than a few old rags or scraps of newspaper.

Long after the war was over and the border controls had been relaxed, this officer happened to meet the young man who had been smuggling in sackloads of contraband during the war, and he said: 'Now that the emergency is over, and all that nonsense about smuggling has been forgotten, can you please tell me what it was you were smuggling over the border all those years?'

'Certainly,' the young man said and, after a long pause, he added: 'Wheelbarrows.'

12

⚘⚘⚘

Διρloματιc Διversions

By 1944, the Irish were cooperating with the British in a way that nobody not in the know – either in Ireland or the United Kingdom – could have possibly imagined. As Tim Pat Coogan puts it in his biography of de Valera:

> Furthermore, as the war continued, the Irish showed a marked consideration and hospitality in areas such as the treatment of downed Allied fliers, who were cared for and speedily transferred across the border. A fiction was created whereby they were regarded as being on 'non-operational' missions and should therefore not be interned. German fliers, however, wound up in the Curragh internment camp and stayed there, whereas around the middle of 1944 the Irish were not even making a pretence of holding

Allied personnel. Cooperation between British and Irish forces eventually progressed to the stage where de Valera appointed his son, Vivion, as liaison officer with General Franklyn, the Commander of British Troops in Northern Ireland. Franklyn and the Irish Chief of Staff, General Dan McKenna, coordinated their strategies at meetings in Annamoe, Co. Wicklow.

Nevertheless, the continuing existence on Irish territory of both a German and a Japanese Legation remained a sore thorn in British and American flesh, which became more and more painful as the launch of Operation Overlord – as the D-Day invasion of the European continent was called – approached.

An earlier attempt by the German Government to increase the staff of its Legation in Dublin (by two officers and one radio operator) almost immediately after the outbreak of war – 'in view of Dublin's increasing importance as an observation post', as the request put it – had already led to an extremely tense situation.

Around Christmas 1940, Ribbentrop was putting heavy pressure on the Irish Government – through William Warnock, Ireland's Chargé d'Affaires in Berlin – to agree to this increase in the Legation personnel, making the 'request' at a time when a plane carrying the extra staff was already in the air and on its way to Rineanna, today's Shannon Airport. De Valera called for an immediate general alert of all the defence forces and ordered that, if the aircraft did land, any Germans it contained were to be immediately arrested and interned. As it happened, the plane could not land because, as part of the cooperative measures agreed with the British, the runways at Rineanna had been blocked. So it flew in low over the airport, the pilot saw the obstructions on the runways and flew straight back to Germany.

During the period of close cooperation between neutral Ireland and the Allies which followed, the British had supplied the Irish with some armaments including some badly needed anti-aircraft guns and some less essential tin hats – one motive for this was the general British dislike of the German-style helmets worn by the Irish army. However, the atmosphere between the Irish and the Germans began to cool early in 1944. Irish intelligence had discovered that the Germans had been transmitting radio messages from Bettystown, Co. Meath – a seaside resort to the north of Dublin, and not all that far south of the border with Northern Ireland. This episode ended with the seizure of the apparatus and its incarceration in a safe in a branch of the Munster and Leinster Bank in Dublin on 21 December 1943. Eduard Hempel, the German Ambassador, and the Irish Department of External Affairs each held a set of keys; and neither was allowed to open the safe except in the company of the other.

On 21 February 1944, David Gray, the US Ambassador to Ireland, called on de Valera, bearing a note requesting:

. . . that the Irish Government take appropriate

steps for the recall of the German and Japanese representatives in Ireland. We should be lacking in candour if we did not state our hope that this action will take the form of a severance of all diplomatic relations between Ireland and these two countries. You will readily understand the compelling reasons why we ask, as an absolute minimum, the removal of these Axis representatives, whose presence in Ireland must inevitably be regarded as constituting a danger to the lives of American soldiers and to the success of the Allied military operations.

De Valera's first reaction was to ask: 'Is this an ultimatum?' Gray replied that it was not, pointing out that it did not contain any direct or implied threat. De Valera then gave his immediate verbal reply: 'As long as I am here, my answer to this request must be no.'

Since at this stage it was pretty certain that the Germans were about to lose the war in Europe, and before very long – and de Valera had had this on the best authority from his own Chargé d'Affaires in Berlin, William Warnock – and since it was also equally clear that the Germans and Japanese had now demonstrated to the entire world that they were on the side (if you could put it that way) of the forces of darkness, you would think that de Valera might have relaxed his fiercely formal stance and gone along with the Allies, but he wasn't made that way. Dev – who may well have seen in the whole situation an opportunity to increase his popularity in the polls by once again standing firm in the face of a challenge to Ireland's independence and sovereignty – resolutely refused to have anything to do with what was, in all conscience, a fairly reasonable suggestion in the circumstances.

On the following day, when presented with the same request by the British Representative in Ireland, Sir John Maffey, he replied: 'This is an ultimatum. This is an outrage.' According to Tim Pat Coogan, de Valera first tried to cause a split between Gray and Maffey by stressing the good working relationship he and Maffey had hitherto enjoyed, by contrast – implied rather than stated – with the strained relationship existing between himself and David Gray. When Maffey failed to fall for that one, Dev changed his tune and took the attitude that the note was an attempt to deprive Eire of both her neutrality and her independence.

He knew very well that one of David Gray's motives in sending the note – aside from the hope of getting rid of the two legations in Dublin, an objective shared with Maffey – was to put the Irish in the wrong in the eyes of the American people. And he decided to defeat Gray's aims in this direction by blatantly treating the note as if it *were* in fact an ultimatum. According to the *New York Times*: 'All leaves in the Irish Army were cancelled immediately, special guards were placed over airfields, ports and other strategic positions. Bridges leading from Ulster into Southern Ireland were mined and the Irish Local

Defence Volunteers were mobilised and armed.' The article went on to say that the Cabinet held marathon sittings, the Defence Council was summoned and informed of the turn events had suddenly taken and, despite his dislike of the whole notion of Dominion status, Dev had called in the Canadian High Commissioner, John Kearney, to enlist the help of the other Dominions in having the notes immediately withdrawn.

Kearney could see no reason why the German and Japanese diplomats should not be expelled, and furthermore was able to confirm – on the authority of both Ottawa and London – what de Valera already knew very well: that American policy towards Ireland was still governed by the statement made by Roosevelt in 1942, at the time when the US troops first arrived in Northern Ireland, a statement which guaranteed that there would be no aggression whatever against Ireland.

De Valera told Kearney that the notes implied a direct threat to which Eire would react. Any interference with the sovereignty of Eire would be stoutly resisted, and the army and country would fight. He intended to summon the Dail, he said, and receive their ratification for the renewal of the ancient struggle, this time, 'if necessary, against England, against America, against everybody'.

Speaking in Cavan on 27 February, he said: 'At any moment the war may come upon us and we may be called upon to defend our rights and our freedom with our lives. Should the day come we will face our duty with the traditional courage of our race.'

Two days later David Gray had another session with de Valera, to pass on to him formally what had already been said to Ireland's representative in Washington, Robert Brennan: that there was no question of an American invasion of Eire.

On 11 March, de Valera published the text of the American and British notes simultaneously with his own lengthy reply which gently hinted that the Americans had been misinformed about 'the uniformly friendly character of Irish neutrality in relation to the United States' and went on:

They [the Government] felt, moreover, that the American Government should have realised that the removal of representatives of a foreign state on the demand of the Government to which they are accredited is universally recognised as the first step towards war, and that the Irish Government could not entertain the American proposal without a complete betrayal of their democratic trust. Irish neutrality represented the united will of the people and parliament. It was the logical consequence of Irish history and of the forced partition of national territory.

On 13 March, Britain banned all travel to and from Ireland: Irish workers then in England would have to remain there indefinitely for military reasons (as it happened, only until after the D-Day invasion had been successfully accomplished, though this was never stated).

In the Commons the next day, Churchill said that measures had been taken to restrict the security risks posed by the existence of the Axis missions in Dublin and added:

. . . the restrictions on travel announced in the press yesterday are the first step in the policy designed to isolate Great Britain from Southern Ireland, and also to isolate Southern Ireland from the outer world during the critical period we are now approaching. I need scarcely say how painful it is to us to take these measures in view of the large numbers of Irishmen who are fighting so bravely in our armed forces and the many deeds of personal heroism by which they have kept alive the martial honour of the Irish race. No one, I think, can reproach us for precipitancy. No nation in the world would have been so patient.

More restrictions followed. There were rumours of complete isolation; all phones were to be cut and all border posts closed, the newspapers reported. On 5 April, Britain did withdraw telephone services to all parts of Ireland, and imposed a ban on the export of all daily and weekly newspapers from England to Ireland. On 17 April, Britain announced that it was to censor all diplomatic bags, and that the departure of official couriers from Britain had been banned. The

High Commissioner for Eire was, for the moment, effectively under house arrest; he was not allowed to travel away from his home in London.

The effect of all this was, of course, enormously to strengthen de Valera's political position, and it would be grossly naïve to pretend that he was not very well aware of this, struggling along as he was in a minority situation. With his back to the wall yet again, facing overwhelming odds, he could always count on the support of the Irish people; all he needed now was an opportunity to call a snap general election. He did not have very long to wait.

The seriousness with which the Irish Government was approaching the whole question of the national-isation of public transportation in Eire had been revealed on 1 January 1944, when legislation for the compulsory acquisition of the DUTC (Dublin United Tramway Company) was introduced, as part of a plan to put all public transport in Ireland under a central government-controlled authority. But some skulduggery over the sale of shares in the old GSR (Great Southern Railway) company on the Stock Exchange towards the end of 1943 had led to a strong feeling among the Opposition that the Fianna Fail party was trying to put something across on them. When the year opened, a Government Tribunal of Inquiry into the whole question of the disposal of GSR stocks was in progress.

Suddenly, at this stage of the proceedings, William T. Cosgrave (who had succeeded Arthur Griffith as first President of the Executive Council of the Irish Free State, and was now leader of Fine Gael, the main Opposition party in the Dail) decided to retire; he was succeeded by General Richard Mulcahy, who had been Michael Collins's deputy Chief of Staff during the final stages of the War of Independence and the Civil War.

In April 1944, it was revealed that a new state-sponsored company, CIE (Coras Iompair Eireann, literally 'the organisation for the carrying of Ireland') was to be formed with a capital of £20,000,000. This would incorporate the GSR and the DUTC, as well as a number of small privately-owned bus companies up and down the country, and a great deal of the privately-owned road transport.

On 3 May, during the second reading of a Transport Bill introduced to put these plans into effect, the Opposition accused the Government of trying to rush the bill through Parliament before the report of the Tribunal had been published, and on 10 May the Government was defeated by one vote (64 to 63) on a motion to defer the Transport Bill until the report of the Tribunal had appeared. In a fit of pique, some said – others knew perfectly well that he was fully aware of what he was doing – Dev called a snap election, ignored all calls for a 'national' coalition government such as they had in Britain, and on 2 June won a resounding victory: a comfortable majority of 14 over all other parties combined.

Amidst all the confusion over the dispatch of the German and Japanese diplomats early in 1944, de

Valera had remained very active in an attempt to save Rome from destruction. Mussolini had fallen in July 1943, and the Allies had invaded Italy in September. The Irish Government petitioned both the British and the Americans to refrain from bombing Rome. In the event, the city was spared from any major damage, but far less as a result of the efforts of Mr de Valera than because by then it didn't appear to the Allies to be a pressing strategic necessity to bomb Rome.

Probably as a result of increasing pressure on neutral Eire – imposed by Churchill, now far more for punitive correctional reasons than, as earlier, to promulgate in Ireland a general climate of fear and dependence which would render the Irish more susceptible to British influence – shortages of essentials went from bad to worse. On 7 June, Sean Lemass, Minister for Supplies, broadcast to the nation, announcing drastic new electricity restrictions. All tram services had already ceased; there was no more coal for many industries; domestic electricity for lighting was cut to one-fifth of the 1941 consumption, and for cooking by one half, and water-heating by electricity was banned altogether; cinemas were to cut programmes to one a day; Radio Eireann programmes were to be curtailed to save electricity; the National Library would be forced to reduce the opening hours of the reading room, and even permanent waves would have to be 'rationed'.

But life went on, and on 21 February the Lord Mayor of Dublin opened the Naas by-pass road, the first dual-carriageway to be constructed in Ireland. Once the Allied Invasion Forces had established themselves firmly in Normandy and were clearly en route for Paris and Berlin, Britain relented on supplies of essential supplies to Eire, in particular coal, and as early as 19 July the Government was able to announce a relaxation of the recent restriction on the use of electricity.

On 18 May, it was announced that VD had become such a problem in Dublin that almost all the city hospitals were arranging to devote special wards to the treatment of sexually acquired diseases. The City Medical Officer of Health reported that the incidence was now 75 per cent higher than in 1941. The general feeling was that the loosening of morals which accompanied every war had somehow spread to Ireland and, in a pastoral letter to his flock, the Rev. Dr Browne, Bishop of Galway, regretted the arrival in his diocese of certain undesirable persons, including prostitutes, for the annual Galway Race Week.

By now the first flying bombs had started to fall on London and the Home Counties, and Churchill told the Commons that 2,752 people had been killed and 8,000 wounded by the new device; the evacuation of London had been resumed. By 12 July, 90 Irish children evacuated from London because of the V-bombs arrived in Dun Laoghaire. The same month, penicillin was produced for the first time in Dublin in the botanical section of the College of Science, Upper Merrion Street.

The Archbishop of Dublin, Dr Charles McQuaid – who had collaborated very closely with de Valera in framing the 1937 Constitution of Ireland which recognised the 'special position' of the Catholic Church as the religion of the majority of the people of Ireland and expressly ruled out divorce in any circumstances – announced in his Pastorals that no Catholic could attend Trinity College, Dublin without his permission, and that any Catholic who disobeyed this dictate was guilty of a mortal sin and while he (or she) persisted in this disobedience was unworthy to receive the sacraments.

The House of Commons was informed on 5 December that there were now 223 Germans and three Japanese interned in Ireland. The Germans were mainly seamen whose ships had been wrecked off the Irish coast or torpedoed in Irish waters, and airmen who had either baled out over Irish territory or whose planes had crash-landed in Eire. Mostly interned at the Curragh Camp in Co. Kildare, they appear to have been model prisoners who, not surprisingly, showed no inclination to escape. Parole was generous (daily anywhere in the Kildare-Kilcullen-Newbridge area and weekly to Dublin) and there was rarely any trouble. The Irish had long since given up trying to intern British airmen in the Curragh, partly because of the special arrangements between neutral Ireland and the Allies, mentioned above, and partly because it was impossible to keep them in captivity in a country where they spoke the language and knew how easy it was to get to the mail-boat at Dun Laoghaire or to cross the border into Northern Ireland.

When first interned, the German prisoners had received regular payments through the German Embassy in Dublin, but by the end of 1944 – with the Allies well-established in France and the Russians on their back doorstep – Berlin had more important matters on its mind than the welfare of a few German internees in neutral Ireland. When they were receiving regular payments, the German internees had kitted themselves out in suits made to their own design from a special brown whipcord unavailable elsewhere in Ireland; the jackets had the full belt of a German shooting jacket, like an overcoat, and the internees were sufficiently determined to have the local Newbridge tailors make their suits precisely as they would have been made in Leipzig, Hanover and Munich.

By the end of 1944, these men were so poor that they were prepared to do any odd job in the camp area in order to earn a few bob. About eighty of them were working regularly on the bog, cutting turf alongside Irish turf-cutters. Another fifty or so were working on the neighbouring farms, cutting hedges and digging ditches. Some, who had managed to acquire a little technical expertise, repaired farm machinery. They kept very much to themselves, and never made friends with the natives.

Patrick Campbell paid a visit to the Curragh to interview them for his column, *An Irishman's Diary*, and reported that when he asked one of them if he would like a drink, the boy replied: 'I do not mind what I have – anything.' Campbell went on: 'He did not seem very ready to talk to a stranger. He was prepared to take any kind of hospitality, whatever it might be, but in a reserved way, without any show of gratitude.'

Paris had fallen to the Allies on 23 August, and two days later the Germans had surrendered, de Gaulle and the Free French forces had occupied the city and taken over the government of France. Joseph Walshe, Secretary of the Department of External Affairs in Dublin, who was as stiff and unyielding in his attitude to protocol as de Valera himself, informed the Free French envoy in Dublin that Eire was prepared to recognise the Gaullist administration 'as the *de facto* government of France'. This caused another temporary coolness between the Allies and neutral Ireland and was particularly resented in the Quai d'Orsay. When Sean Murphy, the Irish envoy to France – based in Vichy, the capital of the Pétain-controlled area, during the German occupation – returned to Paris, the French foreign ministry made it clear that they did not wish to receive him, but Walshe, refused to replace him. Murphy was allowed to remain in France, and eventually met de Gaulle and got on extremely well with him; and on 24 October, the Gaullist Government was fully and formally accepted by the Irish Government without any reservations. In October, too, the Irish Red Cross Society appointed

Colonel T. J. McKinney to form a hospital unit in France; this was set up early in 1945 at St Lo.

At Christmas, there was plenty of gas and electricity for cooking but no fruit with which to make plum puddings, mince pies or cakes. And as the year came to an end, and it looked as if the war in Europe was also drawing to a close, just to show the rest of the world that they were still on active service, those members of the Irish community still dedicated to removing every last relic of British domination from the Irish scene celebrated Christmas by sawing the head off a handsome mounted statue of General Gough in the Phoenix Park on 24 December.

13

ᘓᘓᘓᘓ

The Last Word?

By the final year of the war, the Irish, though still suffering from all kinds of shortages great and small, were doing better than they had ever done since the state was founded. Despite differences with their next-door neighbour over such matters as de Valera's refusal to send the Axis representatives packing, the British continued to take all the food that Ireland could produce. For over five years, Ireland had been supplying all its surplus agricultural produce to the UK, and – with virtually no competitors in the field – at highly favourable prices.

On 1 January 1945, CIE, the state-sponsored road and rail transport monopoly, came into existence, backed by government capital of £20,000,000 (£660, 000,000 today). The Government was prepared to spend another £20,000,000 (£660,000,000) on a programme of total rural electrification which would bring electricity to every farmhouse in the country within ten years. On 1 March, the Government issued a White Paper outlining a £100,000,000 (£3,300,000,000) five-year post-war plan for reconstruction and industrial development and Sean Lemass, Minister for Industry and Commerce, announced that it was proposed to spend yet another £3,500,000 (£115,500,000) on a hydro-electric scheme for the River Erne.

The Turf Development Board had made so much progress on the industrialisation of the industry that they were able to release a documentary film on machine-won turf in April; before the end of the year, the old Turf Development Board was dissolved and yet another new state-controlled company, Board na Mona (Board of the Turf) was set up with a government capital injection of £4,000,000 (£132,000,000) to extend turf production and concentrate on machine-won turf. The Dublin Corporation approved a site in Store Street, near the Customs House, for a very modernistic central bus terminus designed by Michael Scott, to be known as the Busarus (Irish for Bus House), and in April de Valera received a letter expressing the Pope's gratitude at the Irish Government's grant of £100,000 (£3,300,000) for the relief of distress in Italy.

More significantly, perhaps, the Government's financial accounts for the year ended 31 March 1945 disclosed that for the first time ever, income tax receipts at £12,517,000 comprised the biggest contribution to the Exchequer, with customs duties totalling £11,293,000 coming second. Since the foundation of the state, the chief contribution to the Exchequer's annual receipts had always come from customs duties, import taxes and levies of various kinds on imported goods. These figures indicated that the Irish people were not only earning more money, but were at long last beginning to pay their taxes. All around, despite superficial shortages, there were signs of increased prosperity. Towards the end of 1944, at a period when yachting in Britain was a mere memory, seven Dublin professionals and businessmen commissioned a new class of 24-foot (waterline) racing cruisers from Alfred Mylne of the Isle of Bute on the Clyde, the designer of the famous Dublin Bay 21-footers; they cost £1,000 each (equivalent to about £33,000 today). In 1944, too, two *Irish Times* reporters – Des Fricker and I – had bought a yacht; not a very grand one, in all conscience, but even at the beginning of the war the idea that two newspaper reporters (regarded in Dublin as among the lowest forms of animal life) could pay £150 (worth about £4,950 today) for a sailing boat would have been unthinkable.

But despite all this material success, the attitude of Mr de Valera and the Irish hierarchy had not changed one whit. In February, the text of a discussion between de Valera and the St John Ambulance Brigade was published; Dev had apparently recommended that the brigade be amalgamated with the Irish Red Cross Society, as the constitution of the brigade and its continuing connection with Britain 'could not be justified'.

Also in February, the ban on Trinity College, Dublin and on mixed marriages was reiterated in the Lenten regulations of the Archbishop of Dublin, Dr McQuaid, and Cardinal McRory drew attention to the proposed educational reconstruction in the United Kingdom which would apply also to Northern Ireland, stating that conscience forbade Catholics to allow their schools to be placed under state management. Later in the year, de Valera turned his attention to the Royal National Lifeboat Institution and requested them to drop the word 'Royal' from their title; the RNLI's answer was a threat to withdraw all lifeboats from its Irish stations.

However, it was on 2 May that de Valera committed what many people – in Ireland as well as all over the world – considered to be his greatest gaffe to date; on that day he called on Dr Hempel, the German Ambassador in Eire, to express 'his condolence' on the death of Adolf Hitler, which had been reported in that day's newspapers. He did this against the advice of both Walshe and Boland, secretary and assistant secretary of the Department of External Affairs, and defended his action in a letter to Robert Brennan, the Irish representative in Washington:

I have noted that my call on the German Minister on the announcement of Hitler's death was played up to the utmost. I expected this. I could have had a diplomatic illness but, as you know, I would scorn that sort of thing . . . So long as we retained our diplomatic relations with Germany, to have failed to call upon the German representative would have been an act of unpardonable discourtesy to the German nation and to Dr Hempel himself.

The British Representative, Sir John Maffey, was far less critical of de Valera than one might have expected. He thought it unwise but 'mathematically consistent', and felt that de Valera's action might have been partly prompted 'by the most recent assault on his principles', the request from the British and Americans that the keys of the German Legation in Dublin be handed over to them before Hempel had time to destroy the archive material held there.

The fact that the copies of the daily newspapers 'which had contained the account of the death of Hitler in his bunker in Berlin had also contained stories of the atrocities, pictures from Buchenwald, etc.' Maffey felt emphasised the foolishness of de Valera's action: 'A sense of disgust slowly manifested itself,' he remarked in a letter to the Dominions Office about the affair.

May 8 was celebrated as VE Day in Dublin as it was everywhere else; except that in Dublin the celebrations took the form of riots during the course of which windows were smashed in Jammet's Restaurant at the bottom of Grafton Street, Dublin; Trinity College students flew the Union Jack from the roof of the university and set fire to the Irish tricolour, an action which brought retaliation from some students of UCD – among them a future Taoiseach, Charles J. Haughey – who publicly burnt the Union Jack in College Green. There were scenes of wild disorder all over the city.

On the same day the German Legation in Dublin 'was vacated', as the newspapers tersely put it, and on 12 September its furniture and fittings fetched only £1,760 at an auction in Belfast.

On VE Day, too, R.M. Smyllie, editor of the *Irish Times*, played the card he had been holding up his sleeve for the final *coup de grâce* in his battle with the censors. On the evening of 7 May, the Censor went through all the *Irish Times* galley proofs. If he noticed anything odd, it might have been the unusually high proportion of single-column portraits of the Allied war leaders, but it was only to be expected that Smyllie would want to print pictures of the war heroes in the moment of victory, and in any case it was no business of his. When the early, country edition appeared, these single-column pictures appeared at random, scattered throughout the front page. It was an unusual, scrappy sort of layout, but not in any way objectionable from the Censor's point of view.

However, when the final city edition appeared, Smyllie had personally re-made up the front page, arranging the single-column photographs in the form of an enormous V for Victory, spread right up and down from the top to the bottom of the page, across all seven columns.

There was nothing the Censor could do about it. In the final moment of victory, Smyllie had played the trump card.

On 11 May, press censorship was terminated.

The previous day, 10 May, the Minister for Defence, Oscar Traynor, had told the Dail that the cost of demobilising the armed forces would not be less than £4,000,000 (£132,000,000). Dublin Corporation later announced that the cost of removing the 695 air-raid shelters which had been built in Dublin – and never used – would not be less than £59,365, (£1,959,045), a figure which did not include the cost of restoring the roadways. Furthermore, the operation would require 70 gallons of petrol per shelter – a total of 48,720 gallons.

In the course of his victory speech on 13 May, Churchill returned to one of his favourite themes: de Valera's refusal to hand back the Treaty Ports when the Battle of the Atlantic was at its height:

> Owing to the actions of Mr de Valera, so much at variance with the temper and instincts of thousands of Southern Irishmen who hastened to the battle-front to prove their ancient valour, the approaches which the Southern Irish ports and airfields could so easily have guarded were closed by the hostile aircraft and U-boats. This was indeed a deadly moment in our life, and if it had not been for the loyalty and friendship of Northern Ireland we should have been forced to

come to closer quarters with Mr de Valera or perish for ever from the earth. However with a restraint and poise to which, I say, history will find few parallels, His Majesty's Government never laid a violent hand upon them, though at times it would have been quite easy and quite natural, and we left the de Valera Government to frolic with the Germans and later with the Japanese to their heart's content.

De Valera deliberately delayed making any reply for three days, knowing, as the *Irish Press* reported, that it was 'the most eagerly awaited public pronouncement in many years'. In Dublin, the streets were deserted as the time for the broadcast drew near. Neighbours congregated in each others' homes to share the experience, crowding round the radio. In pubs and dance-halls, as the hour approached, the public address systems were tuned to Radio Eireann.

After a brief introduction in Irish, and a long and wordy review of the years of The Emergency and the events of the war, deliberately drawn out to heighten the suspense, de Valera came at last to the bit everybody was waiting to hear:

Mr Churchill makes it clear that in certain circumstances he would have violated our neutrality, and that he would justify his action by Britain's necessity. It seems strange to me that Mr Churchill does not see that this, if accepted, would mean that Britain's necessity would become a moral code and that when this necessity became sufficiently great, other people's rights were not to count.

It is quite true that other Great Powers believe in this same code – in their own regard – and have behaved in accordance with it. That precisely is why we have had the disastrous succession of wars – World War Number One and World War Number Two and, shall it be, World War Number Three?

Surely Mr Churchill must see that if his contention be admitted in our regard, a like justification can be framed for similar acts of aggression elsewhere and no small nation adjoining a Great Power could ever hope to be permitted to go its own way in peace?

It is indeed fortunate that Britain's necessity did not reach the point when Mr Churchill would have acted. All credit to him that he successfully resisted the temptation which, I have no doubt, many times assailed him in his difficulties and to which, I freely admit, many leaders might easily have succumbed. It is indeed hard for the strong to be just to the weak, but acting justly always has its rewards . . .

Mr Churchill is proud of Britain's stand alone, after France had fallen, and before America had entered the war. Could he not find in his heart the generosity to acknowledge that there is a small nation that stood alone, not for one year or two, but for several hundred years, against aggression; that endured spoliations, famines, massacres in endless succession; that was clubbed many times into insensibility but each time, on returning consciousness, took up the fight anew; a small nation that could never be got to accept defeat and has never surrendered her soul?

Once again, Dev had managed to have the last word.

14

⁂

AFTERMATH

De Valera's speech was applauded in most Irish households as a very reasonable response to Churchill's attack on him, and probably about the only one he could have made in the circumstances. It may be, as Tim Pat Coogan suggests, that in certain quarters the reactions were more rapturous.

Cheering, he says, broke out all over the city as Dev finished his broadcast. But I don't remember any cheering, and I was there. When Dev appeared outside the radio station in Henry Street – coincidentally, or possibly intentionally – sited right on top of the GPO headquarters which had been the main command post and focus of the 1916 Easter Rebellion, a large crowd (Coogan says) jostled his protecting Gardai aside to shake his hand and congratulate him (Well, maybe, I wasn't there). The telephone in his office rang all night with messages of congratulation (it would; from the party faithful). He got a standing ovation when he entered the Dail the next day (that is certainly true), and the *Irish Times* commented: 'The Taoiseach's broadcast reply to Mr Churchill was as temperate as it was dignified. Mr de Valera has his faults as a statesman and as a politician; but he has one outstanding quality. He is a gentleman.'

According to Coogan, Winston Churchill's son Randolph told Frank Gallagher, head of the Irish Government's Information Bureau, that his father hadn't liked it one bit . . . 'and was very quiet for a long time after it was delivered'. Coogan also quotes Maffey, writing to the Dominions Office permanent under-secretary, Sir Eric Machtig: '. . . Mr de Valera assumed the role of elder statesman and skilfully worked on all the old passions in order to dramatise the stand taken by Eire in this war. So long as he can work his mystique over Irishmen in all parts of the world Mr de Valera does not have to worry about the rest of humanity.'

Nevertheless, remembering the period as I do, I can't help recalling the feeling that as soon as the euphoria over de Valera's speech had died down – and I don't deny for a moment that it did cause a general euphoria, and very nearly cancelled out the bad taste left in everybody's mouth by his insistence on calling on the German Ambassador to express his 'condolences' upon the death of Adolf Hitler – it was replaced by a general feeling of slight shame, engendered mainly by the release of those dreadful pictures of Belsen and Buchenwald and the slow but general realisation of the horrors which had been perpetrated during the Nazi regime.

Nor was anybody in Ireland too comfortable when William Joyce (Lord Haw-Haw of 'Jairmany calling, Jairmany calling') was arrested near the Dutch border on 29 May. Born in New York, of an Irish father, he had been educated at the Jesuit School in Galway. He was found guilty of treason, was held in the Tower of London and hanged there on 1 January, 1946.

Francis Stuart, who was married to Iseult, daughter of Maud Gonne (MacBride), and in whose house at Laragh, near Glendalough, the German spy Hermann Goertz had spent a few days, had also been broadcasting to the British from Germany during the war. He turned up in Paris in August 1945 and went to the Irish Legation there, where Sean Murphy, the Irish representative, gave him £15 and, according to Dermot Keogh's *Twentieth-Century Ireland: Nation and State*, he was left in no doubt that 'his conduct in 1940, at a particularly dangerous moment of our history, had not been forgotten in Dublin', and that he would not be welcome in Ireland. He was eventually allowed to return to Ireland in 1959.

Charles Bewley, another Irishman on the loose on the European continent during the war, was picked up by the British in Merano, in Northern Italy, towards the end of May 1945, and taken to a prison camp in Terni. He had in fact posed as the Irish Minister both to Berlin and Rome, and carried visiting cards bearing both of these titles, though actually he was working for a Swedish news agency which was part of Goebbels's propaganda machine. It was decided – between Joseph Walshe, Secretary of the Department of External Affairs, and Sir John Maffey – that the best punishment for Bewley would be to demonstrate how unimportant he was by releasing him with a kick in the pants and letting him make his own way back to Ireland. No charges were brought against him, and after his release he continued to live in Italy and died in Rome in 1969.

The after-effects of Ireland's neutrality continued for many years to hamper her in her attempts to integrate with the big outside world. Although supported by both the British and the Americans, de Valera, who had made such a decisive mark on the League of Nations, had to wait until 1955 before Ireland was accepted as a member of the United Nations, though to be fair this was far more a reflection of the profound Soviet Russian mistrust of Roman Catholic countries than anything else. Ireland was very quickly accepted as a full member of a number of the organisations sponsored by the United Nations, including the World Health Organisation and UNESCO, the educational, scientific and cultural branch.

In the Department of External Affairs, Walshe was replaced by his deputy F.H. Boland, who later became Secretary-General of the United Nations at one of the most crucial periods in its history: the time of the confrontation between Khrushchev of the USSR and the entire Western world, when the cast of characters included such diverse and intrinsically difficult characters as Eisenhower, Nehru, Macmillan, Tito, Nasser, Sukarno, Nkrumah and Fidel Castro.

Almost immediately after the war ended, Fianna Fail had to face an electoral challenge.

But first there was the matter of the Presidency. Early in the year – on 5 January, to be precise – Douglas Hyde had indicated to de Valera that he did not propose to seek re-election as President. This decision enabled de Valera to rid himself of a loyal though at times difficult and tactless deputy – it was Sean T. O'Kelly who boasted, after the Economic War, that the Irish had horsewhipped John Bull 'right, left and centre' – and at the same time provide Fianna Fail with an almost unbeatable candidate.

Fine Gael chose a former chief of staff of the Free State Army, General Sean MacEoin, a decent but not very bright member of the human race, and the Independents put their money on Dr Patrick McCartan, an independent republican who had worked as a barman in Philadelphia and was a close associate of McGarrity's in the American Clan na Gael; he was also the man responsible for bringing part of the Russian Crown Jewels to the States as collateral for a $25,000-loan advanced by de Valera to Communist Russian representatives in Washington. He was now a doctor and practised in Co. Tyrone.

When voting took place on 14 June, none of the three candidates secured enough first preferences on the first count to be elected; on the second count, O'Kelly emerged as the victor with 565,165 votes to

MacEoin's 453,425. The diminutive but moderately popular Sean T. O'Kelly was subsequently inaugurated with enormous pomp, accompanied on his passage through the streets of Dublin in an open landau by the army's latest acquisition: a troop of mounted hussars, wearing pale blue uniforms with heavy frogging and a spare jacket worn over one shoulder, not to mention shakos, for all the world like characters out of a 1920s musical comedy about old Vienna. I have good reason to remember every single moment of that day-long, night-long ceremony. I had spent the previous day and the entire night with two friends and my future wife trying to sail a boat from Howth to Dun Laoghaire in a flat calm. Owing to a combination of bad seamanship, poor yacht maintenance (there was a forest of seaweed clinging to the hull below the waterline) and the extremely light airs, it had taken us from around 3 p.m. on Sunday afternoon until 8 a.m. on Monday morning to make the journey (average crossing time between Howth and Dun Laoghaire, say, about three hours) and I had to go straight to the first ceremony of the O'Kelly inauguration in my sailing clothes. Later I snatched opportunities to slip home for a few moments to change first into a formal dark blue lounge suit, and later into full evening dress, white tie and tails, for Sean T. O'Kelly's final transmogrification from a junior assistant in the National Library of Ireland, and a messenger boy during the 1916 Rising, into the President of what was very soon – though due to no action on the part of the bold Sean T. nor his boss Eamon de Valera – to become the Republic of Ireland.

The period of austerity which followed the return to peace in Britain was reflected in Ireland – as, indeed, all fluctuations in the British economy in those days were reflected – and delayed de Valera's and Sean Lemass's plans for continuing industrialisation. Partly because the government in office always gets the blame for any period of austerity, and partly perhaps because they had been in office continuously since 1932, de Valera's Fianna Fail party now began to lose the support of the electorate.

At a general election in 1948 he was returned, still with the biggest party but without a clear, overall majority; he had 68 seats as against 79 held by all the Opposition parties combined.

By then there was a widespread desire for a change of government, both within Parliament and in the country as a whole. To achieve this, all the other parties banded together into a coalition with nothing more in common than an overwhelming desire to get de Valera out and themselves in, which they succeeded in doing with fairly disastrous results. The coalition included such diverse elements as the old Cosgrave party – Cosgrave himself, as we have seen, had retired during the war and been replaced by General Mulcahy, Michael Collins's deputy Chief of Staff – and a new rabidly Republican Party under Sean MacBride, son of Major John MacBride (one of the executed leaders of the Easter 1916 Rising) and of Maud Gonne. The new party, Clann na Poblachta

(Clan of the Republic) stood for a kind of social radicalism quite new to Ireland, as well as a return to the old idea of implacable republicanism. That the old Cosgrave party, now known as Fine Gael (pronounced Finna Gale, it means the Irish race), which for years had upheld the Commonwealth connection with almost indecent zeal, should join forces with a party dedicated to a more extremist republican policy than even Mr de Valera's own is curious enough; that the Labour party and the few Independents and farmers in the Dail should unite to solemnise this most unnatural marriage was even stranger.

Yet it happened, and I was there in the Dail on the night when it happened. My fondest recollection of that evening was that when Dev's final defeat came, Frank Fahy, the speaker, gently reminded the deputies that after Mr de Valera had been up to Arus an Uachtarain to hand in his seal of office, and after Mr Costello – a Dublin lawyer chosen by the Opposition as Taoiseach because he had played no part, honourable or dishonourable, in the Civil War – had been up to receive his seal of office from the President, the deputies who for the past fifteen years had been sitting on the right-hand (Government) benches should be careful to take their places on the left-hand (Opposition) benches. Fahy was obviously afraid that after over fifteen years in power, Dev would automatically return to his old, familiar seat.

But the strangest thing of all was the ultimate fruit of that unnatural marriage: the declaration of the Irish Republic on Easter Monday, 1949.

De Valera had gone to some trouble in his Constitution of 1937 to avoid actually declaring the country an independent republic, partly because he felt that such a declaration would render even more permanent the division between North and South, and partly because he was anxious to hang on to whatever slight advantages there might be in the loose association with the Commonwealth which he had maintained. Now, without any warning, Costello announced that he was going to break the final tie with the Commonwealth, and incidentally with the Six Counties of Northern Ireland, and declare a republic. It might be that he wanted to go down in history as the man who finally set Ireland free, or possibly he was subjected to some pressure by Sean MacBride and his republican supporters. Yet another explanation is that the whole thing was done in a fit of pique. In 1948 Costello was in Canada, attending a Commonwealth Bar Association conference. The conference members were entertained one evening, so the story goes, by the Governor-General of Canada, Field-Marshal Earl Alexander of Tunis, an Ulster Protestant from Co. Tyrone. Alexander, who never had a great deal of time for the southern Irish, did not speak a word to Costello who, it is said, left the dinner in a rage, called the newspapers and announced his intention to cut the last ties with the British Commonwealth. Supporters of Costello claim that as a barrister he had seen so many young men lose their lives or their liberty for their dream of a republic that he decided to give it to them in the hope that it would end all this waste.

Whatever the explanation, the decision to introduce legislation to carry the Republic into effect put Mr de Valera and his party in a bit of a quandary. They did not want a republic declared on this basis, but equally they couldn't very well oppose it. Bob Briscoe, one of the Fianna Fail back-benchers of the period, who advanced the 'fit of pique' theory in his book, *For the Life of Me*, put it this way: 'The Dail ratified Costello's unilateral declaration. We had to. He had made us look foolish enough in the eyes of the world without the stupidity of disowning our own Prime Minister.'

The declaration of the Republic on Easter Monday 1949 aroused no great enthusiasm or excitement in Ireland. There were fireworks in the Phoenix Park the previous evening and a military parade on Easter Monday at which the old women who normally sell flowers and fruit in Moore Street did a brisk trade, shouting 'Get your new Republican colours', which, one couldn't help noticing, were precisely the same as the old Free State colours and those of de Valera's Eire.

Becoming a republic brought about no changes whatever to life in Ireland. Citizens of the Republic could still live, work and vote in the United Kingdom, and British citizens could do the same in the Republic. Questions relating to Ireland were still dealt with by the Commonwealth Office. The currency remained tied to sterling. And Irish travellers arriving at British ports and airports found that they were still treated, willy-nilly, as British subjects.

There was only one respect in which Costello's bid for immortality materially affected the issue between Ireland and England, and that was to render even more permanent the border that divided the Republic from the Six Counties of Northern Ireland. The declaration of Costello's Republic was greeted in England – and by a Labour Government too, although the Labour Party had always leaned in the direction of Irish unity – with the Ireland Act, 1949, a new and explicit guarantee to the Northern statelet. It said, among other things:

> that it is hereby declared that Northern Ireland remains a part of His Majesty's dominions and of the United Kingdom and it is hereby affirmed that in no event will Northern Ireland or any part thereof cease to be a part of His Majesty's dominions and of the United Kingdom without the consent of the Parliament of Northern Ireland.

Northern Ireland does not have a parliament at the moment, but there is no doubt that that guarantee will feature very prominently in the all-party talks on the future of the Six Counties, if they ever get off the ground.

SOURCES AND ACKNOWLEDGEMENTS

The principal source of the material in this book is memory, verified and amplified by recourse to the newspapers of the period at the British Newspaper Library at Colindale. I have also consulted a number of books on various aspects of the subject, all of which are identified in the text. But I would particularly like to thank Tim Pat Coogan for permission to quote passages from two of his books, *The IRA* (London: Pall Mall, 1979) and *De Valera: Long Fellow, Long Shadow* (London: Hutchinson, 1993). The latter contains some fascinating detail about de Valera's diplomatic dealings with the British and Americans which, so far as I am aware, has never appeared elsewhere. The former is the only authoritative and comprehensive history of the IRA in existence, and as such proved invaluable. I would also like to thank Dr Garret FitzGerald for permission to use a couple of extracts from his autobiography, *All in a Life* (Dublin: Gill & Macmillan, 1991); and Mr Bernard Share for permission to use an extract from his own account of the period, *The Emergency: Neutral Ireland 1939–45* (Dublin: Gill & Macmillan, 1978), and I must add that this book proved extremely useful to me as an overall record of the period, with a wealth of detail all the more remarkable for the fact that he was not in Ireland during the war years.

If people who have read my book *Mr Smyllie, Sir* find certain passages in this book uncannily familiar, I make no apology for that; having described the events concerned to the very best of my ability in *Mr Smyllie, Sir*, I saw no reason to make changes just for the sake of making changes.

Tony Gray
Kew Gardens
December 1996

INDEX

McMullan, H. W., 12
McNamar, Brinsley, 112
McNeela, Paddy, 58, 70
McQuaid, Dr John Charles,
  225, 232
McRory, Cardinal, 232
Meath Hotel, 58
Military Tribunal, 10, 31,
  32, 104, 174, 175
Minerals (Exploration
  and Development
  Company), 190
Molloy, John, 86
Montgomery, Alan, 161
Moran, the Rev. Francis,
  191
Mountjoy Jail, 74, 171
Movita, 200
Muirchu, 49, 180
Mulcahy, General Richard,
  101, 222, 245
Mulcahy, Padraic, 101
Municipal Gallery of
  Modern Art, 202
MV Munster, 46
Munster and Leinster
  Bank, 215
Murphy, Sean, 227,
  241
Myles na gCopaleen, see
  Brian O'Nolan
Mylne Alfred, 231

National Defence Council,
  103

National Library, 52,
  223, 224
National Stud, 204
NBBL (No Bread for
  Breakfast League), 185
neutrality, 3, 6, 13, 32,
  35, 37, 39, 45, 105,
  106, 113, 119, 122, 162,
  217–219, 223
New York Herald Tribune,
  59
New York Times, 217
New York World's Fair,
  42, 57, 154
Newman, Alec, 84, 85, 86,
  87, 88, 89, 92, 93, 99, 109,
  124, 158, 159, 165
Nicholls, Nick, 201
Nichols, Beverly, 199
North Strand (Dublin) air
  raid, 124–130
Norton, William, 192, 206

Oath of Allegiance,
  29, 30, 31
Offences Against the State
  Acts, 10
Oige, An, (Irish youth
  hostels organisation),
  180
Oireachtas, 2, 4
Olivier, Laurence,
  201
Orangemen, 3
O'Broin, Sean, 73

Other best selling Warner titles available by mail:

☐ Ireland this Century	Tony Gray	£7.99
☐ Saint Patrick's People	Tony Gray	£6.99
☐ Walking Through Ireland	Robin Neillands	£5.99
☐ Irish Folk and Fairy Tales	Michael Scott	£6.99

The prices shown above are correct at time of going to press, however the publishers reserve the right to increase prices on covers from those previously advertised, without further notice.

WARNER BOOKS

WARNER BOOKS
Cash Sales Department, P.O. Box 11, Falmouth, Cronwall, TR10 9EN
Tel: +44 (0) 1326 372400, Fax: +44 (0) 1326 374888
Email: books@barni.avel.co.uk

POST AND PACKING
Payments can be made as follows: cheque, postal order (payable to Warner Books) or by credit cards. Do not send cash or currency.

All U.K Orders   **FREE OF CHARGE**
E.E.C. & Overseas   20% of order value

Name (Block Letters) _____

Address _____

_____

Post/zip code: _____

☐ Please keep me in touch with future Warner publications
☐ I enclose my remittance £ _____
☐ I wish to pay by Visa/Access/Mastercard/Eurocard

Card Expiry Date

_____